THEY ARE INDEED A VERY USEFUL CORPS

American Riflemen in the Revolutionary War

Michael Cecere

HERITAGE BOOKS
2007

HERITAGE BOOKS
AN IMPRINT OF HERITAGE BOOKS, INC.

Books, CDs, and more—Worldwide

For our listing of thousands of titles see our website
at
www.HeritageBooks.com

Published 2007 by
HERITAGE BOOKS, INC.
Publishing Division
65 East Main Street
Westminster, Maryland 21157-5026

International Standard Book Number: 978-0-7884-4141-7

Contents

Maps

Acknowledgements

I am grateful to a number of people for their assistance on this project. Marguerite Knickmeyer, my teaching partner and friend, edited the manuscript. One of my former students, Lena Assad, assisted with the maps, while Bryant White, a fellow re-enactor and artist, generously contributed a few of his drawings. Other Revolutionary War re-enactors and researchers, such as Joseph Ruckman, Jim Filipski, Bruce McNeal, Glenn Valis, Patrick O' Kelly, John Rees, Mike Barbieri, Thad Weaver, Glenn Williams, Larry Gorecki, Rich Patterson, John Mills, Todd Braisted, Gary Corrado, Steve Rayner, Richard Stickle, Robert Sulentic, Phil Weaver, Greg Ketchum, Eric Schnitzer, Nils Person, Laurence Todd, Bob McDonald, and Dave McKissack, addressed my questions on various RevWar discussion boards and offered their insight and assistance. My passion for this period stems in large part from my involvement with such people and I'm proud to call many of them friends.

Institutions that provided valuable research help included, the Simpson Library at the University of Mary Washington, the Handley Regional Library in Winchester, Virginia, the David Library in Washington's Crossing, Pennsylvania, and the Library of Congress.

Lastly, I want to thank my wife, Susan, and my children, Jenny and Michael, for their continued support. Although my kids never miss a chance to tell me that my passion for history borders on an obsession, I suspect they think it is neat that their dad is an author.

Introduction

This book is the result of a question I had at a reenactment in Trenton, New Jersey. I was standing in the courtyard of the Hessian barracks, waiting to assemble for battle, when I spotted a couple of riflemen off to the side. They were the only riflemen at the event and I wondered how they would be used in the battle. Would they kick off the fight as skirmishers or would they be thrown into the line with the rest of the troops?

This prompted another question. How were riflemen *actually* used in the battle of Trenton? I knew that riflemen played an important role at Quebec, Saratoga, and King's Mountain and that they had a reputation for being undisciplined soldiers, but beyond that my knowledge of riflemen was pretty sparse. I decided that it was time to investigate the role of riflemen in the Revolutionary War.

Since I was primarily interested in learning about the riflemen who fought under continental establishment, I limited my focus to rifle units (continental and militia) that served under General Washington and/or the American army. This excluded hundreds of riflemen who fought in militia units in the south and west. The one exception was the battle of King's Mountain, where southern riflemen (volunteers and militia troops) defeated a large detachment of Tories in South Carolina. This event warranted inclusion because it was such a decisive rifle battle and because it was an important event in the war.

With my research parameters established, I set about to discover the role of riflemen under General Washington and the American army.

Chapter One

America's First Soldiers: The Independent Rifle Companies of 1775

The call went out on June 14th, 1775. Congress needed riflemen for the army at Boston:

> *Resolved: That six companies of expert riflemen, be immediately raised in Pennsylvania, two in Maryland, and two in Virginia…That each company, as soon as completed, shall march and join the army near Boston, to be there employed as light infantry, under the command of* [General Washington].[1]

These riflemen, the first troops authorized by Congress, were America's original Continental soldiers.

Within days, thousands of musket-men were also incorporated into the army. They differed from riflemen in that their smoothbore muskets were grossly inaccurate. To have any hope of hitting the enemy, musket-men typically fired in massed volleys at 50 to 100 yards. Riflemen, on the other hand, could consistently hit their mark at more than 200 yards. The advantage that rifles had in range and accuracy was negated, however, by their slower rate of fire. Loading a smoothbore musket was easier and faster because the bullet did not have to fit tightly in the barrel. As a result, a good musket-man could fire four rounds a minute.

---

[1] Journals of the Continental Congress, June 14, 1775 (accessed thru the Library of Congress website at www.loc.gov)

It typically took riflemen two to three times longer to load their rifles because the bullets, usually wrapped in a greased cloth patch, had to fit tightly into the barrel in order to engage the rifling (grooves) inside the barrel. This produced a spin on the bullet and helped increase the range and accuracy of the shot. Forcing a lead ball down a rifled barrel was difficult, especially after powder residue built up from previous shots. Another disadvantage of rifles was that, in most cases, bayonets could not be attached to them. Such disadvantages, however, did not dampen the interest of prospective recruits.

Pennsylvania, Maryland, and Virginia easily filled their allotted rifle companies with eager volunteers. Pennsylvania had so many recruits that they raised two additional companies and formed an eight company rifle battalion under Colonel William Thompson.[2] Maryland's two rifle companies, commanded by Captains Michael Cresep and Thomas Price, and the two Virginia companies under Captains Hugh Stephenson and Daniel Morgan, remained independent commands.[3] These companies also had an easy time recruiting men. Virginian Henry Bedinger, a member of Stephenson's company, noted that,

> *Volunteers presented themselves from every direction, in the vicinity of these Towns;* [Winchester and Shepherdstown] *none were received but young men of Character, and of sufficient property to Clothe themselves completely, find their own arms, and accoutrements, that is, an approved Rifle, handsome shot pouch, and powder-horn, blanket, knapsack, with such decent clothing as should be prescribed, but which was at first ordered to be only*

---

[2] Journals of the Continental Congress, June 22, 1775 (accessed thru the Library of Congress website at www.loc.gov)

[3] E.M. Sanchez-Saavedra, *A Guide to Virginia Military Organizations in the American Revolutions: 1774-1787*, (Westminster, MD: Willow Bend Books, 1978), 87

a Hunting shirt and pantaloons, fringed on every edge, and in Various ways. Our Company was raised in less than a week. [Captain] *Morgan had equal success.*[4]

Peter Bruin, a rifleman in Daniel Morgan's company, recalled that the challenge in raising the rifle companies was not in finding enough men, but choosing the best marksmen from all the volunteers.[5]

Most of the rifle companies exceeded the 68 riflemen authorized by Congress. Captain Michael Cresep's company had more than 100 men and Captain Morgan's numbered 96.[6] Few in Congress objected to such patriotic enthusiasm. In fact, some advocated the recruitment of even more riflemen. Virginian Richard Henry Lee bragged that,

This one County of Fincastle can furnish 1000 Rifle Men that for their number make the most formidable light Infantry in the World. The six frontier Counties can produce 6000 of these Men who from their amazing hardihood, their method of living so long in the woods without carrying provisions with them, the exceeding quickness with which they can march to distant parts, and above all, the dexterity to which they have arrived in the use of the Rifle Gun. There is not one of these Men who wish a distance less than

---

[4] Danske Dandridge, "Henry Bedinger to --- Findley," *Historic Shepherdstown,* (Charlottesville, VA: Michie Co., 1910), 79

[5] John Dorman, ed., "Peter Bruin Pension Application," *Virginia Revolutionary Pension Applications, Vol. 12,* (Washington, D.C.: 1965), 3

[6] *My Trip to the Barbecue,* (New York: S. A. Rollo, 1860), 68 & Henry B. Dawson, "General Daniel Morgan, An Autobiography," *The Historical Magazine and Notes and Queries Concerning the Antiquities, History and Biography of America,* 2nd Series, Volume 9, (1871), 379

200 yards or a larger object than an Orange. – Every shot is fatal.[7]

Massachusetts delegate John Adams, excited by the reputation of the riflemen, forwarded reports of their good character to New England:

We are told by Gentlemen here that these Riflemen are Men of Property and Family, some of them of independent Fortunes, who go from the purest Motives of Patriotism and Benevolence into this service. I hope they will have Justice done them and Respect shewn them by our People of every Rank and order. I hope also that our People will learn from them the Use of that excellent Weapon a Rifled barrell'd Gun.[8]

By mid July the rifle companies were en route to Boston and were warmly received along the march. People marveled at their appearance and marksmanship. A resident of Frederick, Maryland noted that,

Capt. Morgan, from Virginia, with his company of riflemen (all chosen), marched through this place on their way to Boston. Their appearance was truly martial; their spirits amazingly elated; breathing nothing but a desire to join the American army and to engage the enemies of American liberties. They were met a mile out of town by three companies, viz: Capt. Price's company of riflemen and...[two] companies

---

[7] James C. Ballagh, ed., *Letters of Richard Henry Lee, Vol. 1,* (New York: Macmillan Co., 1911), 130-131
(Richard Henry Lee to Arthur Lee, 24 February, 1775)

[8] "John Adams to James Warren, July 6, 1775," *Letters of Delegates to Congress: Volume 1, August 1774 – August 1775,* (Accessed through the Library of Congress website at www.loc.gov)

of militia, and escorted a few miles out of town, amidst the acclamation of all the inhabitants that attended them. And yesterday Capt. Price with his company also marched, and surely never were two finer companies raised in any country more determined to conquer or die than those two companies are. [9]

Henry Bedinger, of Captain Stephenson's company, recalled that the riflemen were frequently greeted with cheers and kindness:

We were Met by a Number of Men and Women out of the Country who Brought us churns of Beer, Cyder, and Buttermilk, apples, cheries, etc, etc. We honoured them by firing at our parting. [10]

Captain Michael Cresap's company of Maryland riflemen also drew a lot attention, especially for their attire. One admirer wrote that,

I have had the happiness of seeing Captain Michael Cresap marching at the head of a formidable company of upward of one hundred and thirty men from the mountains and backwoods, painted like Indians, armed with tomahawks and rifles, dressed in hunting-shirts and moccasins; and though some of them had traveled hundreds of miles from the banks of the Ohio, they seemed to walk light and easy, and not with less spirit than at the first hour of their march. Health and vigor, after what they had undergone, declared them to be intimate with hardship and familiar with danger. Joy and satisfaction were visible in the crowd that met them. [11]

---

[9] Dandridge, 95
[10] Ibid. 100
[11] *My Trip to the Barbecue,* 68

Cresep's men dazzled spectators with their marksmenship.

> *A clap-board with a mark the size of a dollar was put up; they began to fire off-hand, and the by standers were surprised, few shots being made that were not close or into the paper. When they had shot for some time in this way, some lay on their backs, some on their breasts or sides; others ran twenty or thirty steps and, firing as they ran, appeared to be equally certain of the mark. With this performance the company were more than satisfied, when a young man took up the board in his hand, not by the end but by the side, and holding it up, his brother walked to the distance and coolly shot into the white; laying down his rifle, he took the board, and holding it as it was before, the second brother shot as the former had done. By this exhibition I was more astonished than pleased. But will you believe me when I tell you that one of the men took the board, and placing it between his legs, stood with his back to the tree while another drove the center?*[12]

The excitement generated by the riflemen did not subside when they reached Boston in late July. The New England troops also gave them an enthusiastic reception. One unidentified American officer noted the high regard shown the riflemen:

> *You will think me vain should I tell you how much the Riflemen are esteemed. Their dress, their arms, their size, strength and activity, but above all their eagerness to attack the enemy, entitle them to the first rank. The hunting shirt is like a full suit at St. James's. A Rifleman in his dress may pass sentinels*

---

[12] Ibid.

and go almost where he pleases, while officers of other Regiments are stopped.[13]

Surgeon's Mate James Thacher, of Massachusetts, was also impressed by the southern troops:

> [The riflemen are] *remarkably stout and hardy men; many of them exceeding six feet in height. They are dressed in white frocks, or rifle-shirts, and round hats. These men are remarkable for the accuracy of their aim; striking a mark with great certainty at two hundred yards distance. At a review, a company of them, while on a quick advance, fired their balls into objects of seven inches diameter, at a distance of two hundred and fifty yards. They are now stationed on our lines, and their shot have frequently proved fatal to British officers and soldiers who expose themselves to view, even at more than double the distance of common musket-shot.*[14]

Over time, such acclaim heightened the already inflated egos of the riflemen. They were excused from most duty and were only lightly reprimanded for military infractions. Jesse Lukins, a rifle officer from Pennsylvania, noted that such treatment undermined discipline:

> *Our camp is separate from all others about 100 yards -- all our courts martial and duty was separate -- we were excused from all working parties, camp guards, and camp duty. This indulgence, together with the remissness of discipline and care in our young*

---

[13] B. Floyd Flickinger, "Captain Morgan and His Riflemen," *Winchester-Frederick County Historical Society Journal, Vol. 14* (2002), 58-59

[14] James Thacher, M.D., *Military Journal of the American Revolution,* (Gansevoort, New York: Corner House Historical Publications, 1998), 31

officers, had rendered the men rather insolent for good soldiers. They had twice before broke open our guard house and released their companions who were confined there for small crimes, and once when an offender was brought to the post to be whipped, it was with the utmost difficulty they were kept from rescuing him in the presence of all their officers -- they openly damned them and behaved with great insolence. However the colonel was pleased to pardon the man and all remained quiet.[15]

The lenient treatment and lack of discipline eventually created serious problems. In September, an attempt by the officers to exercise their authority caused some of the Pennsylvania riflemen to mutiny. Lukins recounted the incident:

On Sunday last, the adjutant having confined a serjeant for neglect of duty and murmuring, the men began again and threatened to take him out. The adjutant, being a man of spirit, seized the principal mutineer and put him in also, and coming to report the matter to the colonel, where we, all sitting down after dinner, were alarmed with a huzzaing and upon going out found they had broke open the guard house and taken the man out. The colonel and lieutenant colonel with several of the officers and friends seized the fellow from amongst them and ordered a guard to take him to Cambridge at the Main Guard, which was done without any violent opposition, but in about 20 minutes 32 of Capt. Ross's company with their loaded rifles swore by God they would go to the Main Guard and release the man or lose their lives, and set

---

[15] Henry S. Commager and Richard B. Morris, *The Spirit of Seventy-Six: The Story of the American Revolution as Told by Its Participants*, (NY: Harper Collins Publishers Inc., 1967), 156-157

off as hard as they could run -- it was in vain to attempt stopping them.

We stayed in camp and kept the others quiet -- sent word to General Washington, who reinforced the guard to 500 men with fixed bayonets and loaded pieces. Col. Hitchcock's regiment (being the one next to us) was ordered under arms and some part of General Green's brigade (as the generals were determined to subdue by force the mutineers and did not know how far it might spread in our battalion). Generals Washington, Lee, and Green came immediately, and our 32 mutineers who had gone about half a mile towards Cambridge and taken possession of a hill and woods, beginning to be frightened by the proceedings, were not so hardened but upon the General's ordering them to ground their arms they did it immediately. The General then ordered another of our company's (Capt. Nagles) to surround them with their loaded guns, which was immediately done and...he ordered two of the ring leaders to be bound. I was glad to find our men all true and ready to do their duty except these 32 rascals -- 26 were convenyed to the Quarter Guard on Prospect Hill and 6 of the principals to the Main Guard.

You cannot conceive what disgrace we are all in and how much the General is chagrined that only one regiment should come from the South and that set so infamous an example: and in order that idleness shall not be a further bane to us, the general orders on Monday were "That Col. Thompson's regiment shall be upon all parties of fatigue [work parties] *and do all other camp duty with any other regiment."* [16]

---

[16] Ibid.

General Washington, perhaps out of gratitude to the Pennsylvanians for coming to Boston, was surprisingly lenient on the mutineers and only fined them 20 shillings each.[17] Lukins noted that further punishment was unnecessary.

> *The men are returned to their camp, seem exceedingly sorry for their misbehavior and promise amendment.[18]*

Lukins hoped that the shameful incident would prompt the officers to amend their own behavior as well:

> *This will, I hope awaken the attention of our officers to their duty (for to their remissness I charge our whole disgrace) and the men being employed will yet no doubt do honor to their provinces, for this much I can say for them: that upon every alarm it was impossible for men to behave with more readiness or attend better to their duty; it is only in the camp that we cut a poor figure.[19]*

General Washington's decree that the Pennsylvania riflemen do their share of fatigue and guard duty extended to the Maryland and Virginia riflemen, too. This policy helped restore discipline among the men and fewer infractions were reported. The improved conduct of the riflemen did not erase all of Washington's concerns, however. In late September he complained to his brother Samuel that,

---

[17] Ibid.
[18] Ibid.
[19] Ibid.

The Riflemen have had very little opportunity of shewing their skill, or their ignorance, for some of them, especially from Pennsylvania, know no more of a Rifle than my horse, being new Imported Irish many of whom have deserted to the Enemy.[20]

Washington's disillusionment with the riflemen was only temporary. Their improved conduct at Boston, coupled with their exemplary conduct at Quebec, eventually reaffirmed his high regard of them.

---

[20] Philander D. Chase, "General Washington to Samuel Washington, 30 September, 1775," *The Papers of George Washington: Revolutionary War Series, Vol. 2,* (Charlottesville: University of Press of Virginia, 1987), 73

A Rifleman in Daniel Morgan's Independent Company

Chapter Two

Quebec

Boston was not the only area of activity for American troops in 1775. In late June, Congress directed General Philip Schuyler to lead an American force from New York into Canada. This decision was partly based on the assumption that French-Canadians would welcome Americans as liberators and help defeat the British.[1] Congress hoped that the capture of Canada would reduce Britain's ability to incite the Indians and also prevent a British attack on the colonies from the north.[2]

The plan called for General Schuyler to lead 2,000 men from Crown Point, New York into Canada. General Washington adjusted the plan to include a second expedition. This second force was to *"penetrate into Canada by way of the Kennebeck River,* [in Maine] *and so to Quebeck...."* [3] Washington informed General Schuyler that he could

> *Very well spare a Detachment for this Purpose of one Thousand or twelve Hundred Men...If you are resolved to proceed...*[with an attack from the direction of Lake Champlain] *it would make a Diversion that would distract Carlton* [the British Governor in Canada]*...He must either break up and follow this Party to Quebeck, by which he will leave you a free Passage, or he must suffer that important place to fall into our Hands, an Event, which would*

---

[1] Journals of the Continental Congress, June 27, 1775

[2] "Richard Henry Lee to General Washington, 29 June, 1775," *The Papers of George Washington, Revolutionary Series, Vol. 1,* 45

[3] "General Washington to Maj. General Philip Schuyler, 20 August, 1775," *The Papers of George Washington, Vol. 1,* 332

13

have a decisive Effect and influence on the publick Interest.[4]

General Schuyler supported Washington's plan and commenced his march northward on August 30th.[5]

In Massachusetts, General Washington organized the second expedition to Canada. Colonel Benedict Arnold led the 1,100 man detachment.[6] It consisted of ten musket and three rifle companies. General Washington's orders specified that only *"active Woodsmen...well acquainted with bateaus"* should volunteer for this service.[7] Captain Daniel Morgan's company of Virginia riflemen and two Pennsylvania rifle companies commanded by Captains William Hendricks and Matthew Smith were selected for the expedition. They joined musket-men from New England and New York.

In mid-September, Colonel Arnold's force boarded ships in Newburyport for the passage to Maine. The expedition set sail on September 19th, and arrived at the mouth of the Kennebec River the next day. They transferred supplies to small boats called bateaux and continued upriver to Fort Western, a French and Indian era fort in present day Augusta. This was the base camp for the expedition, the place where final preparations for the long trip were made.

To avoid bottlenecks at some of the narrow portage passages of the river, Colonel Arnold divided the expedition into four divisions with four different departure times. The first division consisted of the three rifle companies and was commanded by Captain Morgan of Virginia. They started

---

[4] Ibid.

[5] Brendan Morrissey, *Quebec 1775: The American invasion of Canada*, (Osprey Publishing Ltd., 2003), 33

[6] Stephen Clark, *Following in Their Footsteps: A Travel Guide & History of the 1775 Secret Expedition to Capture Quebec*, (Clark Books, 2003), 9

[7] "General Orders, 5 September, 1775," *The Papers of George Washington, Vol. 1*, 473

upriver on September 25[8], but quickly fell behind schedule.[8] Pennsylvania rifleman George Morison noted,

> *The water in many places being so shallow, that we were often obliged to haul the boats after us through rock and shoals, frequently up to our middle and over our heads in the water; and some of us with difficulty escaped being drowned.*[9]

While the men in the bateaux battled the swift current and rocky shoals, the rest of the expedition marched alongside the river. They were frequently called upon to assist with the boats, especially when difficult rapids or waterfalls were encountered. The weather also challenged the men, turning cold and raw. Captain Simeon Thayer noted on September 30th, that *"Last night, our clothes being wet, were frozen a pane of glass thick, which proved very disagreeable, being obliged to lie in them."*[10]

The expedition slowly struggled north, the divisions strung out for miles. On October 7th, the rifle division reached the Great Carrying Place. This was the location of a twelve mile portage route that connected the Kennebec and Dead Rivers. Three ponds linked the path and made the overland trek a bit easier. Nevertheless, hauling the heavy boats and supplies over the rough terrain was a daunting task. The riflemen were given the added responsibility of clearing and improving the path for the detachments to come. Rifleman George Morison described the difficulties they endured:

---

[8] Clark, 31

[9] Kenneth Roberts, *March to Quebec: Journals of the Members of Arnold's Expedition*, (New York: Country Life Press, 1938), 511 (George Morison Journal)

[10] Roberts, 250 (Simon Thayer Journal)

This morning we hauled out our Batteaux from the river and carried thro' brush and mire, over hills and swamps...to a pond which we crossed, and encamped for the night. This transportation occupied us three whole days, during which time we advanced but five miles. This was by far the most fatiguing movement that had yet befell us. The rains had rendered the earth a complete bog; insomuch that we were often half leg deep in the mud, stumbling over all fallen logs...Our encampments these two last nights were almost insupportable; for the ground was so soaked with rain that the driest situation we could find was too wet to lay upon any length of time; so that we got but little rest. Leaves to bed us could not be obtained and we amused ourselves around our fires most all the night...The incessant toil we experienced in ascending the river, as well as the still more fatiguing method of carrying our boats, laden with the provisions, camp equipage etc., from place to place, might have subdued the resolution of men less patient and less persevering than we were...Our gallant officers, who partook of all our hardships left nothing unsaid or undone that might hearten us to the enterprise.[11]

After days of backbreaking work, the riflemen reached the Dead River. The expedition made good progress for a few days, but the weather eventually deteriorated, and the Americans were forced to halt and endure the remnants of a hurricane. Rifleman Joseph Henry described the storm's impact:

---

[11] Roberts, 513-514 (George Morison Journal)

A most heavy torrent of rain fell upon us, which continued all night...towards morning we were awakened by the water that flowed in upon us from the river. We fled to high ground. When morning came, the river presented a most frightful aspect: it had risen at least eight feet, and flowed with terrifying rapidity. None but the most strong and active boatmen entered the boats. The army marched on the south side of the river, making large circuits to avoid the overflowing (river)...This was one of the most fatiguing marches we had as yet performed, though the distance was not great in a direct line. But having no path, and being necessitated to climb the steepest hills and without food, for we took none with us, thinking the boats would be near us all day.[12]

To make matters worse, much of the food was spoiled by the wet weather. Surgeon Isaac Senter noted,

The bread casks not being water-proof, admitted the water in plenty, swelled the bread, burst the casks, as well as soured the whole bread. The same fate attended a number of fine casks of peas. These with the others were condemned. We were now curtailed of a very valuable and large part of our provisions...Our fare was now reduced to salt pork and flour. Beef we had now and then, when we could purchase a fat creature, but that was seldom. A few barrels of salt beef remained on hand, but of so indifferent quality, as scarce to be eaten, being killed in the heat of summer, took much damage after salting, that rendered it not only very unwholesome, but very unpalatable.[13]

---

[12] Roberts, 330 (Joseph Henry Journal)
[13] Roberts, 203 (Isaac Senter Journal)

Arnold's March to Quebec

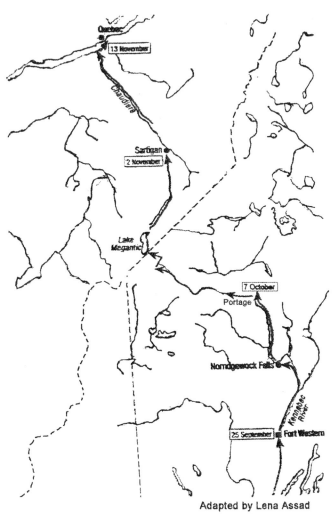

Quebec

13 November

Chaudiere

Sartigan
2 November

Lake
Megantic

7 October
Portage

Norridgewock Falls

Kennebec River

25 September   Fort Western

Adapted by Lena Assad

18

Despite the difficult conditions, the expedition continued onward. On October 25th, a heavy snowfall hit the men, adding to their misery. Dr. Isaac Senter reported,

> *Every prospect of distress now came thundering on with a two fold rapidity. A storm of snow had covered the ground nigh six inches deep, attended with very severe weather.*[14]

Private Morison reported a similar situation, noting in his journal that, *"Last night there fell a heavy snow, and this morning it blew up cold; we suffered considerably this day."*[15]

When the riflemen reached the area known as the Height of Land (the highest point of the march) the two Pennsylvania companies abandoned all but one of their bateaux. The Virginians, however, carried their remaining seven boats over the difficult portage. Joseph Henry described how the Virginians struggled to haul the boats overland:

> *It would have made your heart ache to view the intolerable labors of these fine fellows. Some of them, it was said, had the flesh worn from their shoulders, even to the bone.*[16]

The Virginians were not alone in their suffering. The constant physical exertion and lack of provisions took its toll on all the men. George Morison reported,

> *The time had now arrived when our suffering began to assume a different shape. Famine stared us in the face. Our provisions began to grow scarce, many of our men too sick, and the whole of us much reduced*

---

[14] Roberts, 210 (Isaac Senter Journal)
[15] Roberts, 517-518 (George Morison Journal)
[16] Roberts, 335-336 (Joseph Henry Journal)

by our fatigues; and this too in the midst of a horrid wilderness, far distant from any inhabitation.[17]

A week later, Morison recorded in his journal that,

Never perhaps was there a more forlorn set of human beings...Every one of us shivering from head to foot, as hungry as wolves, and nothing to eat save a little flour we had left, which we made dough of and baked in the fires....[18]

The expedition's ordeal peaked in early November. Dr. Senter recalled,

We had now arrived...to almost the zenith of distress. Several had been entirely destitute of either meat or bread for many days...The voracious disposition many of us had now arrived at, rendered almost anything admissible...In company was a poor dog, [who had] hitherto lived through all the tribulations...This poor animal was instantly devoured, without leaving any vestige of the sacrifice. Nor did the shaving soap, pomatum, and even the lip salve, leather of their shoes, cartridge boxes, &c., share any better fate....[19]

Private Morison had a similar meal on November 2nd:

This morning when we arose to resume our march, many of us were so weak as to be unable to stand without the support of our guns. I myself...staggered about like a drunken man...This day I roasted my

---

[17] Roberts, 515-516 (George Morison Journal)
[18] Roberts, 524 (George Morison Journal)
[19] Roberts, 218-219 (Isaac Senter Journal)

shot-pouch and eat it. It was now four days since I had eat anything save the skin of a squirrel...A number resorted to the same expedient; and in a short time there was not a shot-pouch to be seen among all those within my view...This was the last resort...Hope was now partly extinguished; and its place was supplied with deep insensibility.[20]

The expedition had degenerated into a disorganized band of starving men, scattered along a twenty mile stretch of land. Many fell out of the march, resigned to die in the wilderness. The last three musket companies of the column actually turned back without orders. Yet the rest of the expedition carried on.

Their perseverance was rewarded on November 3rd, when the expedition sighted cattle being driven towards them by an American advance party. The cattle were immediately butchered, and the famished men gorged themselves on fresh beef and other provisions. Many of the rejuvenated men returned to the wilderness to assist their exhausted comrades. Arnold's march through the wilderness was over, but more challenges lay ahead.

On November 14th, Arnold's detachment arrived outside of Quebec. His force was too small to storm the fortified city, but strong enough to commence a siege. This was short lived, however, because Arnold was low on ammunition.[21] On November 19th, he withdrew southward to unite with General Richard Montgomery's force. The two detachments linked up on December 2nd at Point aux Tremble, twenty miles south of Quebec. Montgomery assumed command and promptly returned to Quebec, where he summoned Governor Carleton to surrender. When Carleton rejected the demand the Americans prepared to attack.

---

[20] Roberts, 524 (George Morison Journal)
[21] "Colonel Benedict Arnold to General George Washington, 20 November, 1775," *The Papers of George Washington, Vol. 2,* 403

General Montgomery decided to strike Quebec from two directions and feign an attack from a third. Montgomery led 300 New York troops along the St. Lawrence River toward the lower town of Quebec. They approached from the south. At the same time small detachments demonstrated in front of the western approaches to the town while Colonel Arnold, with 600 men, struck the lower town from the north.[22] Once this section of the town was captured, Arnold's and Montgomery's united force would storm the upper town.

Early in the morning of December 31st, with a winter storm raging, the Americans began their attack. General Montgomery was killed in the early stage of the assault, and his detachment withdrew, leaving Colonel Arnold to storm Quebec alone. Arnold's column, unaware of Montgomery's withdrawal, approached the gates of Quebec through the northern suburbs.

Charles Porterfield, a Virginian rifleman with Captain Morgan's company, recounted the attack in his diary:

We paraded at 4 o' clock, A.M....The signal given, with shouts we set out. In passing by the Palace gate, they fired, and the bells rung an alarm. We marched with as much precipitancy as possible, sustaining a heavy fire for some distance, without the opportunity to return it, being close under the wall.[23]

Rifleman Joseph Henry gave a similar account of the approach:

---

[22] Morrissey, 54-54
[23] "Diary of Colonel Charles Porterfield," *Magazine of American History, Vol. 21,* (April 1889), 318-319

Covering the locks of our guns with the lappets of our coats, and holding down our heads, (for it was impossible to bear up our faces against the imperious storm of wind and snow,) we ran along the foot of the hill in single file...we received a tremendous fire of musketry from the ramparts above us. Here we lost some brave men, when powerless to return the salutes we received, as the enemy was covered by his impregnable defences. They were even sightless to us – we could see nothing but the blaze from the muzzles of their muskets.[24]

As Arnold's detachment continued forward, the advance guard, led by Arnold, became separated from most of the main body. Captain Morgan's rifle company was one of the only units from Arnold's main body that kept up with Arnold. Rifleman Charles Porterfield described what happened:

Coming to the barrier of the entrance of the lower town, guarded by a captain and 50 men, with two pieces of cannon, one of which they discharged and killed two men, we forced them from the cannon, firing in at the port-holes, all the time exposed to the fire of the musketry from the bank above us in the upper town. Here, Colonel Arnold was wounded in the leg and had to retire. The scaling ladders being brought up, if there was any honor in being first over the barrier, I had it. I was immediately followed by Captain Morgan. Upon our approach the guards fled, and we followed close to the guard-house, when, making a halt till some more men should come up, we sallied through into the street. We took thirty men and a captain....[25]

---

[24] Roberts, 375-376 (Joseph Heth Journal)
[25] Porterfield Diary, 319

Daniel Morgan gave a similar account of the attack. With Colonel Arnold wounded and command falling upon him, Morgan recounted,

> I had to attack a two-gun battery, supported by Captain M'Leod and 50 regular troops. The first gun that was fired missed us, the second flashed, when I ordered the ladder, which was on two men's shoulders, to be placed...I mounted myself, and was the first man who leaped into the town, among M'Leod's guard, who were panic struck, and, after a faint resistance, ran into a house that joined the battery and platform...Charles Porterfield, who was then a Cadet in my company, was the first man who followed me; the rest lost not a moment, but spring in as fast as they could find room; all this was performed in a few seconds. I ordered the men to fire into the house, and follow up their fire with their pikes (for besides our rifles we were furnished with long espontoons) this was done, and the guard was driven into the street. I went through a sally-port at the end of the platform; met them in the street; and ordered them to lay down their arms, if they expected quarter; they took me at my word and every man threw down his gun.[26]

The Americans had broken through the first barricade, but in doing so, they were scattered about the lower town. A long delay ensued as Morgan waited for the rest of Arnold's detachment to arrive. "We paraded for some time in the street," recalled Charles Porterfield. "Here we continued for near an hour, before two hundred men got into the barrier,

---

[26] Dawson, 379-380 (Morgan Autobiography)

24

some without officers, and some officers without men, all in confusion....[27]

At the beginning of this delay, Captain Morgan advanced forward to reconnoiter the second barricade. He observed that, *"The sally-port through the barrier was standing open; the guard left it...I found no person in arms at all."* [28] Morgan returned to the first barricade and proposed to the other officers that they continue forward. Morgan recalled,

> *I was overruled by hard reasoning; it was stated that, if I went on, I would break an order, in the first place; in the next place, I had more prisoners than I had men; that if I left them, they might break out, retake the battery, and cut off our retreat; that General Montgomery was certainly coming down the River St. Lawrence, and would join us in a few minutes, so that we were sure of conquest if we acted with caution. To these arguments I sacrificed my own opinion and lost the town.*[29]

Nearly an hour passed before the attack was resumed. During this delay, the British rushed men to the second barrier. As daylight approached, Morgan finally ordered his men forward. Charles Porterfield noted,

> *On approaching the second barrier, [the enemy] hailed us. We immediately fired; they returned it with a shower of shot. Being planted in houses on the opposite side of the barrier, a continual fire ensued for some time, while we rushed up to the barrier, set up our ladder, and, at the same instant, Captain Morgan mounted one, I the other, to force*

---

[27] Porterfield Diary, 319

[28] Dawson, 380 (Morgan Autobiography)

[29] Ibid.

our way, spear in hand, but we were obliged to draw back. Here we were at a disadvantage. Our guns being wet, could not return the fire we were subject to; [we] were obliged to retreat into the street. [30]

Rifleman George Morison also described the assault on the second barricade:

The ladders are laid to the wall – our gallant officers are mounting followed by several men when a furious discharge of musketry is let loose upon us from behind houses; in an instant we are assailed from different quarters with a deadly fire. We now find it impossible to force the battery or guard the port-holes any longer. –We rush on to every part, rouse the enemy from their coverts, and force a body of them to an open fight, some of our riflemen take to houses and do considerable execution. We are now attacked by thrice our number; the battle becomes hot, and is much scattered; but we distinguish each other by hemlock springs previously placed in our hats. All our officers act most gallantly. Betwixt every peal the awful voice of Morgan is heard, whose gigantic stature and terrible appearance carries dismay among the foe wherever he comes. [31]

Despite Morgan's bold leadership, the American situation was critical. *"We are now attacked in our rear,"* wrote Morison, *"the enemy increase momentarily –they call out to us to surrender but we surrender them our bullets..."* [32] Charles Porterfield found cover inside a house where he, fellow

---

[30] Porterfield Diary, 319
[31] Roberts, 537 (Morison Journal)
[32] Ibid. 538

Virginian Peter Bruin, and seven or eight other men continued the fight:

> *We fired...from the windows* [wrote Porterfield] *determined to stand it out or die...Upon seeing Colonel Green and others give up their arms, we held a council what to do, Bruin declaring to the men that, if they thought proper to risk it, he was willing to fight our way out – that he should stand or fall with them.*[33]

While the fight raged at the second barrier, a large British force moved to retake the first one. They encountered Captain Henry Dearborn's musket company who, because of their wet weapons, were unable to offer much resistance. Dearborn's company was overwhelmed and surrendered. With the first barricade back in British hands, Morgan and his men were cut off.

Nevertheless they fought on, hoping that General Montgomery's force would arrive to relieve them. By mid-morning, however, it was evident that Montgomery was not coming and that Morgan's men were trapped. Promised good treatment from their captors, they surrendered in small groups. Daniel Morgan was one of the last to do so, reportedly weeping with anger as he handed his sword, not to the enemy, but to a local clergyman.[34] The battle of Quebec was over and for Morgan and his riflemen, eight long months of captivity lay ahead.

---

[33] Porterfield Diary, 319

[34] James Graham, *Life of General Daniel Morgan*, (Bloomingham, NY: Zebrowski: Historical Services Publishing Co., 1993), 103 (Originally published in 1856)

Quebec

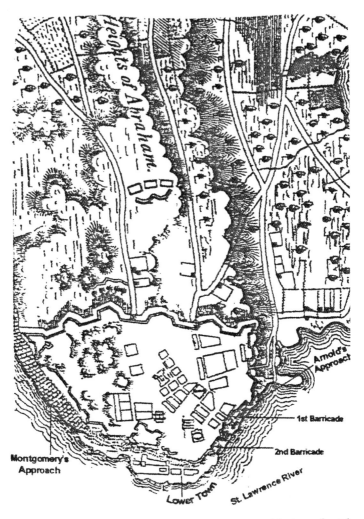

Adapted by Lena Assad

28

Chapter Three

1776

During the fall and winter of 1775, while General Montgomery and Colonel Arnold moved against Quebec, General Washington continued the siege on Boston. In actuality, the siege was more of a stalemate. Earthworks were constructed to protect the Americans from attack and bombardment, but little was done to threaten the British. Washington lacked both cannon and troops to mount a proper siege and concentrated instead on confining the enemy to the town.

The riflemen under Colonel Thompson and Captain Stephenson assisted in this effort. The two Maryland rifle companies and the remaining Virginia company were organized into a loose detachment under Captain Stephenson. They spent the winter in the Roxbury lines. Colonel Thompson's Pennsylvania riflemen were stationed a few miles north, on Prospect Hill.[1] In late October, a detachment of Thompson's rifle battalion was sent to Portsmouth, New Hampshire, to help defend the town. The British had already burnt the coastal town of Falmouth (present day Portland, Maine), and they boasted that Portsmouth was next. Nothing came of these threats, however, and the riflemen had a quiet time in New Hampshire.[2]

The Boston lines were also quiet, with only an occasional outburst of activity. One such incident occurred on November 9th, when Colonel Thompson's rifle battalion, along with American musket-men, skirmished with a large British

---

[1] See: "General Orders, 11 September, 1775," *The Papers of George Washington, Vol. 1*, 449 & Dandridge, *Historic Shepherdstown*, 82
[2] "General John Sullivan to General Washington, 29 October, 1775," *The Papers of George Washington, Vol. 2*, 253

foraging party at Lechmere Point. General Washington described the affair in a letter:

> *On Thursday last about four or five hundred of* [the enemy] *taking advantage of a very high Tide, landed at a place called Litchmores Point (opposite to Boston and then an Island) distance about ¾ of a Mile from our Lines on prospect Hill, but upon the appearance of two Regiments* [including Thompson's Battalion] *advancg towards them, over a Causey (waste deep in Water) they retreated...having first kild & carrd off 10 head of Cattle, but with the loss of two of their Men. We had three Men wounded, two I fear mortally.*[3]

General Washington added in another letter that, "*The alacrity of the Riffle-men & Officers upon that occasion* [Lechmore Point] *did them honor....*"[4]

The approach of winter caused both sides to limit further activities. The focus of General Howe and General Washington shifted to the next campaign season. Each side prepared for what was expected to be a decisive year.

In January, General Washington and Congress restructured the American army. Many of the units, including Colonel Thompson's Pennsylvania rifle battalion, were renamed. Thompson's battalion became the 1st Continental Regiment. Colonel Thompson was promoted to Brigadier General and placed in charge of a brigade, so Lieutenant Colonel Edward Hand assumed command of the Pennsylvania riflemen. The Maryland and Virginia rifle companies remained under Captain Stephenson's command.

---

[3] "General Washington to William Ramsay, 10-16 November, 1775," *The Papers of George Washington, Vol. 2*, 344

[4] "General Washington to Lt. Col. Joseph Reed, 30 November, 1775," *The Papers of George Washington, Vol. 2*, 463

Boston

Adapted by Lena Assad

31

As the siege entered 1776, the Americans grew tired of the standoff. General Washington pondered an attack in February but decided instead to threaten the British by fortifying Dorchester Heights with newly arrived cannon from Fort Ticonderoga. Washington believed placing artillery on these hills would force the British to either attack his fortified position at great loss, or evacuate Boston. On the evening of March 4th, General Washington sent 2,000 men to the heights under cover of darkness. Henry Bedinger, a rifleman from Virginia, described the movement in his journal:

> *Orders Came out to go on Dorchester Point and Intrench, two Rifle-Companies from Cambridge were ordered here. In the Evening as soon as Sun Down our Teams Began to Load with Intrenching Tools, Spears, Canon, about 100 Teams to Carry Facines and pressed Hay, accordingly 2000 men and upwards went and Began the work.*[5]

With cannon on the opposite end of the line blasting away to distract the British, American work parties erected fortifications on Dorchester Heights. General Washington proudly informed Congress of the successful operation:

> *As soon as our firing commenced, a considerable detachment of our men under the command of Brigadier General Thomas crossed the Neck and took possession of the Two Hills without the least interruption or annoyance from the Enemy, and by their great activity and Industry before morning advanced the Works so far, as to be secure against their Shot....*[6]

---

[5] Dandridge, 128

[6] "General Washington to John Hancock, 7-9 March, 1776," *The Papers of George Washington, Vol. 3*, 420

Washington expected the British to try to dislodge his men, so he sent reinforcements, including Stephenson's three rifle companies and two others from Colonel Hand's regiment. They were posted in advance of the fortifications and screened the work parties from enemy attack. Henry Bedinger recalled,

> *About 1 O'Clock our five Companies of Riflemen Marched on, when the Others had already made Two Compleat Facine forts on the Top of the Two Hills, made Two Redoubts and a Cover along the Neck with hay. We marched a Little Beyond the Forts and posted ourselves behind a hill Near the water Edge where we Remained as Silent as possible.*[7]

The riflemen stayed at their post for two days. During this time new American work parties improved the fortifications. Private Bedinger noted,

> *A Vast number of Barrels of Dust and Sand were Set around Each fort on the Top of the Hills in order to Roll Down to Break the Ranks of the Enemy if they offered to attack us, the Riflemen Lay Still at the hill. (The) General [Ward] Requested they should (remain) another Night and Untill the Tide went out on the Next Day which Capt. Stephenson Consented to who Commanded the five Companies provided the Gen'l would send us another Day's provision which he did Next Morning.*[8]

Just as Washington expected, when General Howe learned about the new fortifications on Dorchester, he immediately ordered an attack. In the middle of his preparations, however, a storm struck and delayed the assault. Upon further

---

[7] Dandridge, 128
[8] Ibid. 129

consideration, Howe cancelled the attack and decided to abandon Boston. He informed the Americans of his decision and threatened to burn the town if they interfered.

Washington let the British leave in peace and took possession of the city on March 17th. His stay in Boston was brief, however, because he feared that New York was Howe's next destination. Washington ordered the riflemen to New York before the British boarded their ships. They reached New York at the end of March and were joined by the rest of the army in April.[9]

A Very Useful Corps

General Washington spent the spring and summer in New York preparing for General Howe's return. Efforts were made to re-enlist soldiers whose service was near an end. Washington was particularly interested in retaining the riflemen. Although they were committed to serve through July, Washington urged Congress in mid-April to approve a plan to re-enlist as many riflemen as possible:

> *As the time for which the Rifle men inlisted will expire on the first of July next, and as the loss of such a valuable and brave body of Men will be of great injury to the Service, I would submit it to the Consideration of Congress whether it would not [be] best to adopt some method to induce them to Continue – **They are indeed a very useful Corps**.*[10]

Congress responded and authorized the rifle officers to re-enlist their men for two years. This proved difficult for the officers from Virginia and Maryland. In July, General Washington reported to Congress that,

---

[9] Dandridge, 133
[10] "General Washington to John Hancock, 22 April, 1776," *The Papers of George Washington, Vol. 4*, 105

Only about Forty of the three old Companies have reinlisted, which I shall form into one for the present and place under an Officer or two, till a further and compleat Arrangement is made of the whole Battalion.[11]

The "arrangement" that Washington mentioned was a new rifle battalion consisting of the remnants of the Virginia and Maryland rifle companies and six additional companies raised in Virginia and Maryland over the summer.[12] Colonel Stephenson was placed in charge of the battalion, which was not completed until the fall. Sadly, Stephenson never commanded the battalion. In August, while recruiting in Virginia, he grew ill and died. Lieutenant Colonel Moses Rawlings, of Maryland, assumed command of the new rifle battalion.

The additional rifle companies were not the only new riflemen recruited for the American army; hundreds of riflemen joined continental regiments in Virginia as well. In the beginning of 1776, Virginia raised six regiments to supplement the original two that were raised in 1775. Each of the new two year regiments consisted of seven musket and three rifle companies. The rifle companies served as light infantry and, like the musket companies, numbered sixty-eight men.[13]

---

[11] "General Washington to John Hancock, 4 July, 1776," *The Papers of George Washington, Vol. 5,* 199
[12] Journals of the Continental Congress, 27 June, 1776 (accessed thru the Library of Congress website at www.loc.gov)
[13] William Hening, ed., *The Statutes of Large Being a Collection of all the Laws of Virginia, Vol. 9* (Richmond: J & G Cochran, 1821), 76

Unlike the independent rifle companies, the rifle companies in the Virginia regiments operated as part of each regiment. This came as a surprise to one Virginia rifle officer who was convicted by a court martial in April 1776 of, *"refusing in presence of the whole Battalion to do his Duty as an officer on Parade."*[14] The convicted officer believed that,

> *All officers Commanding Rifle Companies, as they were raised as – Light Infantry...no Commanding Officer has a right to make them do parade Duty.*[15]

This opinion was held by a number of Virginia rifle officers. General Charles Lee, the commander of the southern department, was amazed to learn of such views:

> *The idea hatched by some of the Rifle Companies that they are not subject to every duty of soldiers, is really a curious one, more especially, when we consider that more than one half of the Virginian Troops are composed of Riflemen; at this rate, the Musqueteers would have a blessed time of it, to make the system consistent and compleat, the latter ought to black the former's shoes, and wash their shirts.*[16]

Although General Lee dismissed the idea of preferential treatment for the riflemen, it is unclear whether they actually drilled with the musket companies. Rifles were weapons that emphasized accuracy over firepower. Rifle tactics centered on individual marksmanship rather than massed volleys, so it is

---

[14] "Major Spotswood to General Charles Lee, 11 April, 1775," *The Lee Papers, Vol. 1,* (Collections of the New York Historical Society, 1871), 412

[15] Ibid. 412-413

[16] "Charles Lee to Major Spotswood, 15 April, 1776, *The Lee Papers, Vol. 1,* 423

A Rifle Officer of the
Virginia Line

doubtful that riflemen would have spent a lot of time practicing volley fire.

On the other hand, there is little evidence, in the form of orderly books or letters, to support the view that riflemen were treated differently than musket-men in the Virginia regiments. The 1776 orderly books of the 5th and 6th Virginia regiments show no distinction between musket and rifle companies. Numerous orders call for "the troops" and "the companies" to parade and drill, and nothing is mentioned to suggest that riflemen were excused from such activities.[17]

Virginia was not the only colony to send rifle reinforcements to General Washington; Pennsylvania also recruited more riflemen. Pennsylvania addressed the difference between musket-men and riflemen by raising distinct battalions of each. A state rifle regiment, commanded by Colonel Samuel Miles, was recruited in the spring. It consisted of two battalions of riflemen and one musket battalion. Each battalion numbered around 400 men.[18] The regiment was posted outside of Philadelphia until July, when it was ordered to join Brigadier General Hugh Mercer's Flying Camp in New Jersey.

The Flying Camp was established by Congress in early June 1776, to act as a reserve force for General Washington's army in New York. It was supposed to consist of 10,000 men from Pennsylvania, Maryland, and Delaware, but frequent requests from General Washington for reinforcements limited

---

[17] See: *The Order Books of the Company of Captain George Stubblefield Fifth Virginia Regiment From March 3 to July 10, 1776*
(Accessed at www.revwar75.com)   and
    Charles Campbell, *The Orderly Book of that Portion of the American Army stationed at or near Williamsburg, Virginia under the command of General Andrew Lewis, from March 18th, 1776 to August 20th, 1776,*
(Richmond, VA: 1860)
[18] Charles Lesser, ed., "A Return of the Army...July 27, 1776," *The Sinews of Independence: Monthly Strength Reports of the Continental Army,*
(Chicago: The Univ. of Chicago Press, 1976),   26

its size. In the summer of 1776, the bulk of the Flying Camp was stationed near Amboy, New Jersey.

Defending New York

While the colonies scrambled to recruit more men, General Washington prepared to defend New York. Virginia rifleman John Cole recalled that in April,

> *Three volunteer companies of riflemen were sent to Staten Island to prevent the inhabitants from trading with the British fleet which was coming in and anchoring below the light.*[19]

A week after their arrival, the riflemen skirmished with a British watering party from the British sloop, *Savage*. Private Cole recalled,

> *On Easter Sunday the Savage sloop of war came up for the purpose of procuring water on the island. They were informed of it by some of the inhabitants. A part of the three companies gathered and went down upon them, took seventeen prisoners, a musket, a stand of colors, a twelve yard barge, 27 water casks, buckets and funnels.*[20]

Richard Boucher, another Virginia riflemen in Stephenson's company, proudly claimed,

---

[19] John Dorman, ed., "John Cole Pension Application," *Virginia Revolutionary Pension Applications, Vol. 20*, (Washington, D.C., 1974), 85
[20] Ibid.

The riflemen alone drove them off, killed a number, took thirteen prisoners with their flag, and caused the sloop of war...to cut her cable and bear off, losing both her barge and anchor.[21]

Across the narrows from Staten Island, Colonel Edward Hand's continental rifle regiment (formerly Thompson's Battalion) guarded Long Island. The regiment was attached to General Nathanael Greene's brigade and, like the whole army, anxiously awaited the British. Colonel Hand's three hundred men had a busy summer on Long Island.[22] When the main portion of the British invasion fleet arrived in July, Colonel Hand was ordered to keep watch on their activity. He sent daily reports to General Greene, who forwarded them to General Washington on Manhattan Island.

The enormous British force worried General Washington and prompted him to call for reinforcements. On August 8th, Washington wrote to Colonel Samuel Miles, the commander of the Pennsylvania state rifle regiment, for assistance:

We have Reason to expect an early & very vigorous Attack for which we would wish to have more equal Numbers: Upon looking round I do not see any Quarter from which I may so confidently look for Assistance as the Pennsylvania Troops who have shewn so much Spirit & Zeal & particularly those of the three Battalions under your command of whom I hear a most excellent Character.[23]

Washington worried that by the terms of their enlistment the Pennsylvanians, who were in New Jersey with General

---

[21] John Dorman, ed., "Richard Boucher Pension Application," *Virginia Revolutionary Pension Applications, Vol. 8*, (1963), 68

[22] Lesser, "A Return of the Army...July 27, 1776," 26

[23] "General Washington to Colonel Samuel Miles, 8 August, 1776," *The Papers of George Washington, Vol. 5*, 635-636

Mercer's Flying Camp, might refuse to march to New York. He therefore appealed directly to their patriotism:

> *I do not scrutinize with the Terms of the Inlistment of Troops at such a Time as this, nor would I avail myself of any Authority derived from that Source. Brave Men who love their Country and are resolved to defend it, will go where the Service requires at so critical and dangerous a Period as this and Men of a different Character, such I hope we have not among us, can be useful no where. I flatter myself therefore when the brave Officers and Soldiers under your special Command reflect that the Time is fast approaching which is to determine our Fate and that of our Posterity they will most chearfully persevere and comply with such Requests respecting their March and Destination as the State of Things requires. Under this Perswasion I have wrote to General Mercer to desire one of the Riffle Battalions may be forwarded over as we have not one Corps of this Kind in or near New York, and the Ground in many Places will admit them to act with great Advantage.*[24]

Washington's appeal had the desired effect. General Mercer informed him the next day that,

> *In consequence of your Excellencys Letter – Col. Miles will march with all his Riflemen – The two Battalions will make about 700.*[25]

The Pennsylvanians arrived in New York on August 11th. After a two week stay on Manhattan Island, they were ordered to Long Island. This was in response to British troop landings

---

[24] Ibid.

[25] "Brigadier General Hugh Mercer to General Washington, 9 August, 1776," *The Papers of George Washington, Vol. 5,* 651

41

at Gravesend Bay, about ten miles from the American lines in Brooklyn. Sergeant James McMichael, a member of the rifle regiment, recorded in his journal that,

> *The enemy having landed on Long Island, our brigade was paraded and ordered thither. After leaving our camp, the order was modified – one half to proceed to Long Island, the remainder to follow at a moment's notice. The First Battalion together with our musketry, and the Delaware Blues, went to the island and we* [the 2nd rifle battalion] *were ordered to our tents.*[26]

McMichael's rifle battalion crossed over to Long Island the next day and spent a difficult night in the field. He reported in his journal that, *"This night we camped in the woods, without tents, in a hard rain. Sentries firing all night."*[27]

Battle of Long Island

The British invasion of Long Island began at sunrise on August 22nd, when 15,000 British and Hessian troops landed at Gravesend Bay.[28] General William Howe, the British commander, sent a large detachment inland to seize the village of Flatbush and probe the American defenses.

Colonel Edward Hand's Continental riflemen were nearby and deployed in advance of the British detachment. They withdrew, however, prior to an engagement. As the

---

[26] "Diary of Lieutenant James McMichael of the Pennsylvania Line, 1776-1778," *The Pennsylvania Magazine of History and Biography, Vol. 16, No. 2* (1892), 133
(Henceforth referred to as McMichael Diary)
[27] Ibid.
[28] Henry P. Johnson, *The Campaign of 1776 Around New York and Brooklyn*, (New York: Da Capa Press, 1971), 140
(Originally published in 1878)

Pennsylvanians retreated, they burned stacks of grain and hay and killed cattle to deny them to the enemy.[29] At one point the riflemen attempted to ambush the British. Lieutenant Colonel James Chambers described the affair in a letter to his wife:

> *When we came on the hill we discovered a party of them* [the British] *advancing toward us. We prepared to give them a warm reception, when an imprudent fellow fired, and they immediately halted and turned toward Flatbush.*[30]

In New York City, General Washington was concerned by reports that only 8,000 enemy troops were on Long Island. This meant that thousands more were not yet deployed. Washington believed that the landings on Long Island might be a feint to draw the Americans away from General Howe's real target, New York.[31] He expressed this concern to Connecticut Governor Jonathon Trumbell on August 24th:

> *On Thursday last the Enemy landed a body of Troops, supposed to Amount (from the best Accounts I have been able to obtain) to Eight or Nine Thousand Men at Gravesend Bay on Long Island, Ten Miles distance from our Works, (on the Island) and immediately marched thro' the Level and open Lands to Flat Bush, where they are now incamped:-- They are distant about three Miles from our Lines, and have Woods and broken Ground to pass (which we have lined), before they can get to them; some Skirmishing has happened between their Advanced parties and ours, in which we have always obtained an Advantage; what the real Designs of the Enemy*

---

[29] Ibid. 141-142
[30] Ibid. 142
[31] Ibid. 148

are, I am not yet able to determine. My Opinion of the Matter is, that they mean to attack our Works on the Island, and this City, at the same time, and that the Troops at Flat Bush are waiting in those Plains, till the Wind and tide (which have not yet served together) will favor the Movement of the Shipping to this place [New York]. Others think they will bend their principal Force against our Lines on the Island, which if carried will greatly facilitate their designs upon this City. This also being very probable, I have thrown what force I can over, without leaving myself too much exposed here; for our whole Numbers, if the Intelligence we get from Deserters &c. be true, falls short of that of the Enemy.[32]

General Washington's uncertainty about British intentions caused him to send only a limited number of reinforcements to Brooklyn.

The Americans established two defensive lines on Long Island. The main line was a series of earthworks and redoubts along Brooklyn Heights. These heights, which overlooked the East River and New York City, were important for the city's defense. British artillery could shower New York with shot and shell from that position and make the town untenable for the Americans. The other American defensive position on Long Island stretched along a series of hills and ridges in advance of the Brooklyn line. The position, called Gowanus Heights, was heavily wooded and formed a natural barrier between the British and Americans. Roads passed through the heights in a number of gaps, or passes, which the Americans fortified. Each pass was defended by approximately 800 men, and pickets were stationed in the woods between the passes.[33]

---

[32] "General Washington to Jonathon Trumball Sr., 24 August, 1776," *The Papers of George Washington, Vol. 6*,   123
[33] Johnson, 156

44

Long Island

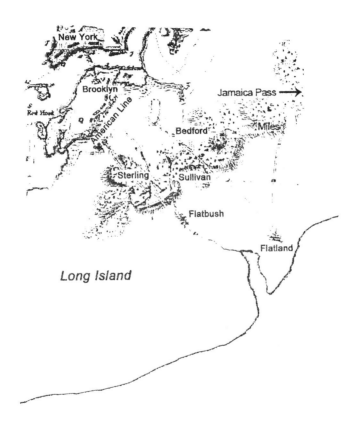

Adapted by Lena Assad

45

The British approached the American line with caution, sending reconnaissance parties forward to probe the defenses. One such probe resulted in a sharp skirmish that involved Colonel Hand's riflemen. American General John Sullivan described the affair to General Washington:

> *This Afternoon the Enemy formed & attempted to pass the Road by Bedford a smart fire between them and the Rifle Men ensued, the Officer sent off for a Reinforcement which I ordered down Immediately, a number of Musketry came up to the Assistance of the Rifle Men whose fire with that of our field pieces caused a Retreat of the Enemy...[34]*

Lieutenant Colonel James Chambers participated in the skirmish and provided more details:

> *Strong guards were maintained all day on the flanks of the enemy, and our regiment and the Hessian yagers kept up a severe firing, with a loss of but two wounded on our side. We laid a few Hessians low, and made them retreat from Flatbush. Our people went into the town and brought the goods out of the burning houses. The enemy liked to have lost their field-pieces...We would certainly have had the cannon had it not been for some foolish person calling retreat.[35]*

The next three days were relatively calm as the British consolidated their forces and prepared to attack. Washington remained anxious about General Howe's intentions and expressed his concern in a letter to his cousin on August 26th:

---

[34] "Major General John Sullivan to General Washington, 23 August, 1776," *The Papers of George Washington, Vol. 6*, 115
[35] Johnson, 147

The Enemy...landed a pretty considerable part of their Force on Long Island...about Ten Miles from our Works on the Island; and Marched...till they (or part of them) got within abt three Miles of our Lines, where they are now Incampd; A wood & broken ground lying between Us. What there real design is I know not...however, I have strengthened the Post as much as I can, to prevent a Surprize, and have lined the Wood between them and Us, from whence some Skirmishes have ensued and lives lost on both sides.[36]

Washington's concern prompted him to send additional reinforcements to Long Island, which increased the number of defenders along Gowanus Heights to almost 1,000 men per pass. Colonel Miles's Pennsylvania state rifle regiment was posted in the woods east of the Bedford Pass. They held the far left flank of the American line. On their left, about two miles away, was another pass through Gowanus Heights. Amazingly, this position, called Jamaica Pass, was unguarded.[37]

Colonel Miles was deeply troubled by the lack of American troops to his left. He expressed his concern to General John Sullivan when the general visited the lines:

I told him the situation of the British Army; that Gen'l Howe, with the main body, lay on my left, about a mile and a-half or two miles, and I was convinced when the army moved that Gen'l Howe would fall into the Jamaica road, and I hoped there were troops there to watch them.[38]

---

[36] "General Washington to Lund Washington, 26 August, 1776," *The Papers of George Washington, Vol. 6,* 136
[37] Johnson, 154 - 160
[38] Johnson, Part 2, "Journal of Samuel Miles", 61

Lieutenant Colonel Daniel Brodhead shared the concerns of his commander, Colonel Miles, and commented in his journal:

Gen'ls Putnam, Sullivan and others came to our camp which was to the left of all the other posts and proceeded to reconnoiter the enemie's lines to the right, when from the movements of the enemy they might plainly discover they were advancing towards Jamaica [Pass], and extending their lines to the left so as to march round us, for our lines to the left, were, for want of Videttes, left open for at least four miles where we constantly scouted by Day, beside mounting a Guard of one hundred men & an advance party of subaltern and thirty to the left of us, was hard Duty for our Reg't....[39]

Major General Israel Putnam had arrived a day earlier to command Long Island's defenses. The lack of troops limited his ability to defend Jamaica Pass. The best he could do was station a few cavalrymen there.

General Howe Attacks

General Howe's battle plan was simple. Two large detachments, commanded by General James Grant and General von Heister, would assault the American held passes at Gowanus Heights to draw Washington's attention to his center and right flank, while a 10,000 man force led by General Henry Clinton and General Charles Cornwallis marched around the American left flank via the Jamaica Pass to strike the Americans in the rear.[40] If all went as planned, the Americans would be crushed between two British forces.

---

[39] Johnson, Part 2, "Lieut.-Col. Daniel Brodhead To ------, 64
[40] Mark Boatner III, *The Encyclopedia of the American Revolution*, (Stackpole Books, 1994), 651

Howe's flanking force commenced its march toward Jamaica Pass early in the evening of August 26th. They reached the pass around 2:00 a.m. and captured the American horsemen posted there.[41]

While the British flanking party secured Jamaica Pass, General Grant advanced his detachment toward the right flank of the American line. The American pickets withdrew up the road and alarmed the encampment at Brooklyn Heights. General William Stirling rushed 2,000 men, including militia riflemen from Pennsylvania under Lieuenant Colonels Peter Kachlein and Nichlolas Lutz, to confront General Grant. Stirling's men took a strong position and halted the British advance. Unbeknownst to them, General Grant was content to employ his artillery to hold the Americans in place until the British right wing enveloped them.[42]

General von Heister began his assault on the center of the American line at 7:00 a.m. The sound of battle caused Colonel Miles and his rifle regiment to leave their position on the left flank and march towards the fight, but they were stopped by a continental Colonel who told Miles that his regiment was needed elsewhere.[43] Miles disagreed. He believed the enemy was marching for the Jamaica Road and convinced the officer to let him march in that direction. Colonel Miles recalled,

After marching nearly two miles, the whole distance through woods, I arrived within sight of the Jamaica road, and to my great mortification I saw the main body of the enemy in full march between me and our lines [at Brooklyn] *and the baggage guard just coming into the road.*[44]

---

[41] Johnson, 176-177
[42] Johnson, 161- 167
[43] Johnson, Part 2 "Journal of Col. Samuel Miles", 61- 62
[44] Ibid. 62

Colonel Miles and the American army were in trouble. The British had flanked their line and were bearing down on their rear. The Pennsylvanians acted quickly to escape the trap. Colonel Miles ordered Lieutenant Colonel Brodhead, the commander of the rear rifle battalion, to retreat and, *"push on by the left of the enemy and endeavour* [to] *get into our lines* [at Brooklyn]."[45] Colonel Brodhead attempted to comply, but his battalion became disordered. He re-formed half of the battalion, but then noticed an American artillery unit struggling with a field piece and ordered his men to help protect it. In the midst of this move, Brodhead's men were again thrown into disorder, this time by retreating American musket troops. Colonel Brodhead recalled,

> *I did all in my power to rally the musquetry & Riflemen, but to no purpose, so that when we came to engage the Enemy, I had not fifty men, notwithstanding which, we after about three Rounds, caused the Enemy to retire, and as the Enemy's main body was then nearly between us and the lines, I retreated to the lines, having lost out of the whole Battalion, about one hundred men, officers included.*[46]

Sergeant James McMichael was attached to Broadhead's rifle battalion and provided more details about their escape:

> *We numbered just 400. We at first thought it prudent to retire to a neighboring thicket, where we formed and gave battle. Here my right hand man fell shot thro' the head. We were attacked by the enemy's left wing, while their right endeavoured to surround us. Their superior numbers forced us to retire for a short distance, when we again formed and fought with*

---

[45] Ibid.

[46] Johnson, Part 2, "Lieut.Col. Daniel Brodhead to ----", 64-65

fortitude until we were nearly surrounded. Having by this time lost a great number of men, we were again forced to retreat, when we found that the enemy had got between us and the fort. Then despairing of making good our retreat we resolved to die rather than be taken prisoners, and thus we were drove from place to place 'till 3 o'clock p.m., when we agreed to attempt crossing the mill-pond, that being the only way left for our escape. Here numbers were drowned, but it was the will of Providence that I should escape, and at half past three, we reached the lines, being much fatigued. The enemy advanced rapidly and endeavoured to force our lines, [at Brooklyn Heights] but were repulsed with considerable loss.[47]

Colonel Miles, with the lead rifle battalion, attempted to follow Brodhead's battalion, but was cut off by the British. Miles recalled,

We immediately began our march, but had not proceeded more than half a mile until we fell in with a body of 7 or 800 light infantry, which we attacked without any hesitation, but their superiority of numbers encouraged them to march up with their bayonets, which we could not withstand, having none ourselves. I therefore ordered the Troops to push on towards our lines. I remained on the ground myself until they had all passed me, (the enemy were then within less than 20 yards of us,) and by this means I came into the rear instead of the front of my command.[48]

---

[47] McMichael Diary, 134
[48] Johnson, Part 2, "Journal of Col. Samuel Miles", 63

Colonel Miles's battalion eventually disintegrated, and he, along with over 150 of his men, was captured.[49]

While these events transpired on the far left of the American line, the rest of the American troops at Gowanus Heights held firm, unaware of the danger to their flank and rear. The shocking news that the British were about to encircle them arrived with the British troops themselves. The American center quickly collapsed and the panicked troops raced for the safety of the Brooklyn lines. Scores of Americans were bayoneted and many more, including General Sullivan, were captured.

All that remained of the American advance line was General Stirling's force on the right. Stirling's men held the British in check all morning, but the sound of combat in their rear worried them. Unaware that the rest of the American line had collapsed, Stirling fought on, unwilling to retreat without orders. He eventually realized his perilous situation. With nearly every avenue of escape to the Brooklyn lines blocked, Stirling ordered his men to break ranks and cross Gowanus Creek as best they could. To buy time for his men, General Stirling personally led an attack against the British with half of the 1st Maryland Regiment. The conduct of the Maryland troops earned them universal esteem and saved hundreds of Americans from capture. The Marylanders with Stirling were not so fortunate. Most of them, along with General Stirling, were captured.

The battle of Long Island was a disaster for the Americans. Yet, the result was less decisive than it could have been. Although he routed Washington's advance line at Gowanus Heights, General Howe approached the main American line at Brooklyn with caution. He decided to avoid a bloody frontal assault and commence a siege instead. This tactic took time and allowed General Washington to withdraw his men to

---

[49] Ibid.

Manhattan Island under cover of darkness. Thousands of American soldiers were saved to fight another day.

Battle of Harlem Heights

After a two week pause, General Howe resumed the offensive. British and Hessian troops landed on Manhattan Island and easily captured New York. Once again, however, they allowed most of the American army to escape, this time to Harlem Heights on the northern end of the island.

The British followed the Americans to Harlem Heights and dug in opposite them. Early the next morning, British troops fired on a detachment of New England rangers who were patrolling between the two lines.[50] The rangers, commanded by Colonel Thomas Knowlton of Connecticut, held their ground for thirty minutes before retiring.[51] The skirmish attracted General Washington's attention and prompted him to take the offensive.

While a detachment of musket-men from the newly arrived 3rd Virginia Regiment advanced to draw the British out of their lines again, the regiment's three rifle companies, commanded by Major Andrew Leitch, and Colonel Knowlton's Connecticut rangers marched around the enemy's right flank to strike them in the rear. Captain John Chilton commanded one of the 3rd Virginia musket companies and described the attack:

> We marched down toward [the enemy] and posted ourselves near a meadow having that to our front, [the North] river to our right, a body of woods in our rear and on our left. We discovered the enemy peeping from their Heights over their fencings and

---

[50] Philip Katcher, "They Behaved Like Soldiers: The Third Virginia Regiment at Harlem Heights," *Virginia Cavalcade, Vol. 26, No. 2,* (Autumn 1976), 64

[51] Ibid.

*rocks and running backwards and forwards. We did
not alter our positions. I believe they expected we
should have ascended the hill to them, but finding us
still, they imputed it to fear and came down skipping
towards us in small parties. At a distance of 250 or
300 yards they began their fire. Our orders were not
to fire till they came near but a young officer...on the
right fired and it was taken up from right to left. We
made about 4 fires ... We then all wiped and loaded
and sat down in our ranks and let the enemy fire on
us near an hour."*[52]

Unfortunately for the Americans, the young officer that
Chilton mentioned was not the only American to fire early.
The flanking force also struck the British early and failed to
gain their rear. Despite this miscue the riflemen and rangers,
joined by the American musket companies, fought with such
tenacity that the British retreated. David Griffith, the
regimental surgeon for the 3rd Virginia, proudly recounted the
affair in a letter home:

*A very smart action ensued in the true Bush-fighting
way....our Troops behaved in a manner that does
them the highest Honor. After keeping a very heavy
fire on both sides for near three hours they drove the
enemy to their main Body and then were prudently
ordered to retreat for fear of being drawn into an
ambuscade. The 3rd Virga. Regt. was ordered out at
the Beginning to maintain a particular post in front,
and Major Leitch was detached with the 3 Rifle
Companies to flank the Enemy. He conducted
himself on this occasion in a manner that does him
the greatest honor and so did his Party, till he*

---

[52] Tyler, Lyon, ed., "John Chilton to friends, 17 September, 1776," *Tyler's
Quarterly Historical and Genealogical Magazine, Vol. 12*, (Richmond,
VA, : Richmond Press, 1931), 93

received two balls in his Belly and one In his hip...We had 3 men killed and ten wounded.... Our whole loss is not yet ascertained. The wounded are not more than 40. Coll. Noleton [Knowlton] of the N.E. Rangers is the only officer killed.... This affair, tho' not great in itself, is of consequence as it gives spirits to the army, which they wanted. Indeed the confusion was such on Sunday that everybody looked dispirited. At present everything wears a different face.[53]

American morale rose after Harlem Heights as reports of fleeing British troops spread through camp. Washington remained at Harlem Heights, while General Howe settled into New York. Although the American position was strong, it was vulnerable to encirclement. The British navy could block the river crossings at any moment, leaving just one crossing point to the mainland at Kings Bridge. It was vital, therefore, that Washington hold the bridge as an escape route off the island.

General William Heath commanded the American troops in the vicinity of King's Bridge. One of his brigades was led by General Thomas Mifflin. After the battle of Long Island, the bulk of the American riflemen, including Colonel Hand's 1st Continental Regiment and the remnants of Colonel Miles's two Pennsylvania rifle battalions, were attached to Mifflin's brigade and posted near Kings Bridge. Colonel Hand's regiment did not sustain many casualties at Long Island and numbered about 300 men.[54] Conversely, Colonel Miles suffered significant losses at Long Island, and was himself captured. Lieutenant Colonel Broadhead succeeded Miles and

---

[53] Henry Johnson, "David Griffith to Major Leven Powell, 18 September, 1776," *The Battle of Harlem Heights*, (London: Macmillian, 1878), 171-172

[54] Lesser, "Return of the Army...September 28, 1776," 32

New York

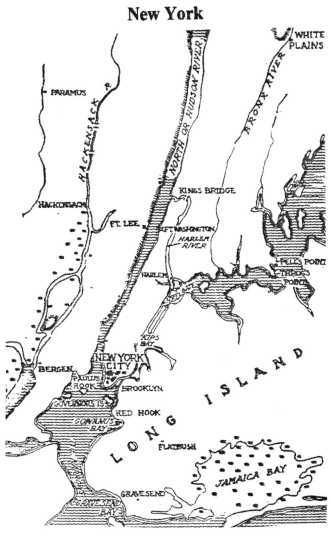

Adapted by Lena Assad

struggled to keep the state rifle regiment intact. Desertion was a major problem. General Heath described one incident to General Washington:

This morning about Ten O' Clock I was informed that one of Col. Broadhead's Battalions of Riflemen had drawn up, & were determined to march home—I immediately ordered several Regiments under Arms, & then road to them...I demanded the Reasons of their Mutinous Behavior; they replied the want of money & Blankets, & the Severe Duty of the Camp; that they were Volunteers &ct. I ordered them immediately to repair to their Tents (or the Severest punishment shou'd be inflicted) which they did in an orderly manner...I am just informed that the other Rifle Battalion of Pennsylvanians are extremely uneasy & talk of going home in a Body, I hope they will be removed this night to the Island [Manhattan].[55]

General Heath received his wish, and the disgruntled riflemen were ordered back to Manhattan Island, but not before over 200 had deserted.[56]

Throg's Neck to White Plains

General Howe finally resumed the offensive on October 12th, and landed a large party of troops on the mainland at Throg's Neck. The British planned to march to Kings Bridge and trap the Americans on Manhattan Island. Howe's choice of a landing site, however, was poor.

---

[55] "Major General William Heath to General Washington, 19 September, 1776," *The Papers of George Washington, Vol. 6,* 342
[56] Ibid. 343 note 2

To reach the mainland from Throg's Neck, one had to pass a creek and marshland that flooded at high tide. There were only two routes over these obstacles; one was a causeway and bridge and the other was a ford near the headwaters of the creek. Both locations were ideal defensive positions, and both spots were covered by Colonel Hand's riflemen. They were placed there a few days earlier by General Heath who recalled in his memoirs that,

> *Our General* [Heath] *in reconnoitering his position, accompanied by Col. Hand, below the camp of the rifle corps, being apprehensive that the British might land on Frog's* [Throg's] *Neck, took a view of the causeway between West-Chester and the point...After taking a full view, our General directed Col. Hand, immediately upon his return to his camp, to fix upon one of the best subaltern officers, and 25 picked men of his corps, and assign them to this pass, as their alarm-post at all times; and, in case the enemy made a landing on Frog's neck, to direct this officer immediately to take up the planks of the bridge.*[57]

Tench Tilghmen, an aide to General Washington, also described the area:

> *Trogs Neck and Point is a Kind of Island, there are two Passages to the Main which are fordable at low Water at both of which we have thrown up works, which will give some Annoyance should they attempt to come off by either of these ways...Our Rifle men have directions to attend particularly to taking down*

---

[57] William Abbatt ed., *Memoirs of Major-General William Heath*, (New York : William Abbatt, 1901),   59
(Originally printed in 1798)

58

their Horses, which if done, will impede their march effectually.[58]

When the British finally advanced towards the mainland, Colonel Hand's riflemen did more than annoy them, they stopped the British dead in their tracks. General Heath described the encounter:

The [British] *troops landed at Frog's Neck, and their advance pushed towards the causeway and bridge, at West Chester mill. Col. Hand's riflemen took up the planks of the bridge, as had been directed, and commenced a firing with their rifles. The British moved towards the head of the creek, but found here also the Americans in possession of the pass. Our General* [Heath] *immediately (as he had assured Col. Hand he would do) ordered Col. Prescott, the hero of Bunker Hill, with his regiment, and Lieut. Bryant of the artillery, with a 3 pounder, to reinforce the riflemen at West Chester causeway; and Col. Graham of the New-York line, with his regiment, and Lieut. Jackson of the artillery, with a 6 pounder, to reinforce at the head of the creek; all of which was promptly done, to the check and disappointment of the enemy. The British encamped on the Neck. The riflemen and Jagers kept up a scattering popping at each other across the marsh; and the Americans on their side, and the British on the other, threw up a work at the end of the causeway. Capt. Bryant, now and then, when there was an object, saluted the British with a field-piece.*[59]

---

[58] "Tench Tilghman to William Duer, 13 October, 1776," *The Papers of George Washington, Vol. 6,* 536 note 3

[59] Heath's Memoirs, 62

By the end of the day, 1,800 Americans faced the British.[60] For five days Howe's men sat at Throg's Neck unable to cross onto the mainland, but unwilling to withdraw. Finally, General Howe moved his troops across a cove to Pell's Neck. This was only a short distance away, but was a much better landing area.

The new American commander on the scene, General Charles Lee, had anticipated this move and placed Colonel John Glover's brigade in the area to contest Howe's advance inland. When the British began their march, Glover's 750 musket-men ripped into them from behind stone walls and trees.[61] Although they were outnumbered more than five to one, Glover's men brought the British advance to a crawl and gave General Washington additional time to re-position the American army.

Washington posted his men in the hills outside of White Plains, New York and awaited the British. His right flank rested on Chatterton Hill, and his left was protected by a creek and pond. General Howe slowly approached with 13,000 men.[62] As they neared the American lines, advance parties from both sides skirmished. One incident occurred on October 23rd, when German riflemen, called Jagers, commanded by Captain Johann Ewald, were ambushed by Colonel Hand's riflemen. Ewald recalled,

We had marched only a few minutes when several shots rang out on our left. As I tried to gain a hill from which I could look around, our left wing suddenly came under fierce fire. With the half of the platoon I had taken with me I rushed toward the sound of the firing, where I found a handful of my jagers engaged with several battalions of Americans.

---

[60] Boatner, 1101
[61] Ibid. 850
[62] Ibid. 1200

I could not retreat, especially as I assumed that I was supported, and I could not advance with my few men, since I caught sight of a camp nearby which must have belonged to the enemy army.

I maneuvered as well as I could to cover both flanks...Suddenly Colonel Donop appeared with a few dragoons and shouted at me to retreat. I replied that I could not do so, because if I abandoned this position the greater part of my company would be captured. He retorted, 'You want to conquer America in one day? You write rules and then violate them.' Thereupon he rode off. Shortly afterward he returned with a battalion of English light infantry with two guns, whose bayonets and grapeshot provided the precious air by which I was saved. I got off with a loss of six dead and eleven wounded...and two taken prisoner.[63]

American Lieutenant Colonel Robert Harrison, an aide to General Washington, also provided a brief account of the engagement:

On Wednesday there was also a small skirmish between a party of Colo. Hands Riflemen (about Two Hundred & forty) & nearly the same number of Hessian Chasseurs, in which the latter were put to the Rout. Our men buried Ten of them on the field & took Two prisoners, One badly wounded. We sustained no loss than having one lad wounded, supposed mortally.[64]

---

[63] Joseph Tustin, ed., *Diary of the American War: A Hessian Journal*, (New Haven : Yale University Press, 1979), 9-10 (Henceforth referred to as Ewald's Journal)

[64] "Lt. Col. Robert Harrison to John Hancock, 25 October, 1776," *The Papers of George Washington, Vol. 7*, 28

Colonel Hand's men were not the only American riflemen to see action at White Plains. On October 21st, Sergeant James McMichael, of the Pennsylvania State Rifle Regiment, noted in his diary that, "*a party of 100 men, properly officered, from our riflemen, left to scour the woods near the enemies lines.*"[65] McMichael reported that the riflemen returned two days later with 35 prisoners.[66] Unfortunately, the Pennsylvanians were also involved in a tragic friendly fire incident. Sergeant McMichael reported that, "*taking the Delaware Blues* [Delaware continental troops] *for the enemy, we fired on each other, in which six of our riflemen and nine of the Blues were killed.*"[67] Despite the loss, the riflemen continued to scout the area. They brought 16 enemy prisoners into camp on October 27th. Twenty-four hours later, the Pennsylvania rifle regiment participated in the battle of White Plains. General Washington sent them forward to confront the British advance. Sergeant McMichael recalled,

> *My regiment was sent to the front to bring on the action, but not to endanger ourselves enough to be taken prisoners. We had not marched two miles before we saw them coming. We were attacked by their right wing (all Hessians) and after keeping up an incessant fire for an hour, we were informed by our flanking party, that their light horse was surrounding us, when we retreated to the lines. Their left wing attacked a party of ours at an advanced post on a hill. Our troops behaved with great fortitude, but being overpowered by numbers, were obliged to fall back to the lines. The enemy attempted to force our right wing in the lines, but were driven back, and finally retreated.*[68]

---

[65] McMichael Diary, 137
[66] Ibid.
[67] Ibid.
[68] Ibid.

Although each side had a large number of troops at White Plains, only a portion fought at Chatterton Hill, the principal area of the battle. Continental troops from Delaware and Maryland, along with militia forces, stubbornly defended the hill and inflicted a number of casualties on the attacking Hessians. The weight of Howe's attack was too great, however, and the Americans withdrew from the hill.

Pleased with the day's gains, General Howe halted his troops and waited for reinforcements. He attempted to resume his advance two days later, but poor weather postponed the move. When the skies cleared on November 1st, General Howe discovered that Washington had withdrawn to an even stronger position five miles to the north. Howe ended his pursuit and returned to New York. Although he was frustrated by his inability to destroy Washington's army, General Howe was determined to strike a decisive blow against the Americans. Fort Washington, on Manhattan Island, provided the ideal target.

Fort Washington

Fort Washington, built on a 230 foot elevation overlooking the Hudson River, was originally constructed to challenge British shipping on the river. It was one component of the American defenses at Harlem Heights. When General Washington moved the bulk of his army to White Plains in mid-October, Fort Washington became the bastion of the reduced American presence on Manhattan. Despite General Washington's doubts about the value and security of Fort Washington, he accepted the advice of General Nathanael Greene and maintained a garrison there. General Greene, who was posted across the river at Fort Lee, explained the importance of Fort Washington in a letter to General Washington:

Upon the whole I cannot help thinking the Garrison [Fort Washington] *is of advantage – and I cannot conceive the Garrison to be in any great danger the men can be brought off at any time ... Col. Magaw* [Fort Washington's commander] *thinks it will take* [the enemy] *till December expires, before they can carry it* [the fort]... *If the Enemy don't find it an Object of importance they wont trouble themselves about it -- if they do, it is full proof they feel an injury from our possessing it – Our giving it up will open a free communication with the Country by the Way of Kings bridge – that must be a great Advantage to them and injury to us.*[69]

Colonel Robert Magaw commanded the 1,200 man garrison at Fort Washington. Although this contingent was adequate to defend the fort, it was far short of the manpower necessary to properly defend the approaches. When Washington realized that Fort Washington was Howe's next objective, he rushed reinforcements there. By mid-November, 2,800 Americans were stationed on Manhattan Island.[70]

Included in that number were approximately 250 riflemen from Virginia and Maryland.[71] They belonged to Colonel Moses Rawlings rifle regiment. Most of the riflemen were new recruits, raised over the summer for Colonel Stephenson's Virginia / Maryland rifle regiment.

The riflemen were posted along the northern approach to Fort Washington. Virginian Henry Bedinger, a veteran of 1775, noted that,

---

[69] "General Nathaniel Greene to General Washington, 9 November, 1776," *The Papers of George Washington, Vol. 7,* 120

[70] Johnson., 277

[71] Boatner, 386

Our Reg't tho weak was most advantageously placed by Rawlings and Williams (Otho) on a Small Ridge, about half a mile above Fort Washington.[72]

The riflemen were joined by musket-men from Maryland and Pennsylvania. Other American troops were stationed in the lines at Harlem Heights and along the Harlem River to resist possible attacks from those directions. Colonel Magaw remained at Fort Washington, which was the fall back position for the troops outside the fort.

Despite American efforts to bolster the defenses around Fort Washington, General William Howe was confident that his three pronged, 8,000 man attack, would overwhelm the rebels. Hoping to avoid bloodshed, Howe summoned the Americans to surrender the fort in mid-November. Colonel Magaw rejected the demand and pledged to defend Fort Washington to the last.[73] The stage was set for one of America's worst defeats of the war.

The British attack began early in the morning of November 16th. Thousands of British and Hessian troops advanced on Fort Washington from three directions. Two thousand men under General Hugh Percy attacked the American lines at Harlem Heights and easily drove the rebels back. Another three thousand British soldiers crossed the Harlem River under General Charles Cornwallis and swept the American militia aside. Both columns converged on Fort Washington.

The situation north of the fort was different. Colonel Rawlings' riflemen and the supporting musket-men waged a spirited defense against 3,000 Hessians. Henry Bedinger recalled,

---

[72] Dandridge, 157

[73] George Scheer and Hugh Rankin, *Rebels and Redcoats: The American Revolution Through the Eyes of Those Who Fought and Lived It*, (Da Capo Press, 1957), 198

*A few of our men were killed with cannon and grape
shot. Not a shot was fired on our side until the enemy
had nearly gained the summit. Though at least five
times our number, our rifles brought down so many
of them that they gave way several times...This
obstinacy continued for nearly an hour.*[74]

Hessian Captain Andreas Wiederhold acknowledged the
difficulty of the assault:

*We stood facing their crack troops and their riflemen
all on this most inaccessible rock which lay before
us, surrounded by swamps and three earthworks, one
above the other.*[75]

John Reuber, another Hessian soldier, also recalled the
difficult fight:

[We] *marched forward up the hill and were obliged
to creep along up the rocks, one falling down alive,
another being shot dead. We were obliged to drag
ourselves by the beech-tree bushes up the height
where we could not really stand.*[76]

The strength of the Hessian attack eventually forced the
riflemen back. Henry Bedinger maintained that,

*Our troops retreated gradually from redoubt to
redoubt, contesting every inch of ground, still making
dreadful havoc in the ranks of the enemy. We
labored, too, under disadvantages, as the wind blew
the smoke full in our faces.*[77]

---

[74] Dandridge, 157
[75] Scheer & Rankin, 199
[76] Henry Steele Commager and Richard B. Morris, ed., *The Spirit of
'Seventy-Six: The Story of the American Revolution as Told by
Participants*, (Edison, NJ : Castle Books, 2002), 494
[77] Dandridge, 157

When the riflemen returned to the fort, the flaw in the American defense became apparent. Hundreds of men milled about, unable to find a position along the earthworks. There were too many men in the fort, and many of them had no shelter against bombardment. A Hessian officer summoned Colonel Magaw to spare his men and surrender. Magaw wanted to hold out until evening and attempt a night withdrawal, but his situation was desperate and he capitulated.

The fall of Fort Washington, with over 2,800 men and a significant amount of supplies, was a major blow to the American army. General Washington acknowledged this in a letter to Congress the day the fort fell:

> *The Loss of such a Number of Officers and Men, many of whom have been trained with more than common Attention, will I fear be severely felt. But when that of the Arms and Accoutrements is added much more so.*[78]

General Howe gave Washington little time to absorb the loss and crossed the Hudson to attack Fort Lee. General Washington abandoned the post and withdrew into New Jersey, leaving most of the American army in New York under Generals Lee and Heath. General Lee had the largest part of the army, nearly 7,500 New England troops, near White Plains. General Heath had approximately 4,000 men to protect the New York Highlands. The remaining American troops, approximately 3,700, were with General Washington in New Jersey.[79] They were mostly "southern" troops from Pennsylvania, Delaware, Maryland, and Virginia and included all the riflemen. Militia from New Jersey and Pennsylvania augmented Washington's force, but they were still vastly

---

[78] "General Washington to the Board of War, 16 November, 1776," *The Papers of George Washington, Vol. 7,* 165
[79] Lesser, " Return of the Army...December 1, 1776," 40-41

outnumbered by General Howe's army and were steadily pushed across New Jersey.[80]

[80] Ibid.

Chapter Four

Washington's Army Rebounds

By late November, General Washington and his men were in serious trouble. Significantly outnumbered by the British, Washington was powerless to stop Howe's advance. Captain John Chilton of the 3rd Virginia Regiment described the American retreat across New Jersey:

> *Our Regmt. brought up the rear. This was a melancholy day, [November 27] deep miry road and so many men to tread it made it very disagreeable marching, we came 8 or 10 miles and encamped....How long we shall stay, I can't say, but expect we shall make a stand near this place [New Brunswick] if not at it, but no certainty when the Enemy are advancing on and an engagement may happen before tomorrow night. We must fight to a disadvantage. They exceed us in numbers greatly.*[1]

Sergeant James McMichael, with the Pennsylvania state rifle regiment, made a similar observation in his diary:

> *Intelligence that the enemy are marching for Brunswick causing us to prepare to meet them but we are reduced to so small a number we have little hopes of victory.*[2]

---

[1] Tyler, "John Chilton to his brother, 30 November, 1776," *Tyler's Quarterly*, 98
[2] McMichael Diary, 139

Luckily for Washington, General Howe's pursuit was sluggish. On December 7th, the Americans reached the Delaware River and crossed over into Pennsylvania.

When the British arrived at the river, they had no way to cross because Washington had collected all the boats in the area. The Americans, scattered along the west bank of the river, scrambled to stay warm and find food. Lieutenant Enoch Anderson of the Delaware Regiment described his first night in Pennsylvania:

> We *lay amongst the leaves without tents or blankets, laying down with our feet to the fire. It was very cold. We had meat, but no bread. We had nothing to cook with but our ramrods, which we run through a piece of meat and roasted it over the fire, and to hungry soldiers it tasted sweet.*[3]

David Griffith, the regimental surgeon for the 3rd Virginia, described the situation on December 8th:

> We *have much need for a speedy re-inforcement. I am much afraid we shall not have it in time to prevent the destruction of American affairs... Everything here wears the face of despondency...A strange consternation seems to have seized everybody in this country. A universal dissatisfaction prevails, and everybody is furnished with an excuse for declining the publick service.*[4]

---

[3] "Personal Recollections of Captain Enoch Anderson, an Officer of the Delaware Regiment in the Revolutionary War," *Papers of the Historical Society of Delaware, Vol. 16,* (Wilmington: The Historical Society of Delaware, 1896), 28

[4] Tyler, "David Griffith to Major Powell, 8 December, 1776," *Tyler's Quarterly,* 101

Even General Washington was concerned. He wrote to his brother on December 18th, that,

> *Our Affairs are in a very bad situation...In a word my dear Sir, if every nerve is not strain'd to recruit the New Army with all possible expedition, I think the game is pretty near up.*[5]

For almost three weeks, Washington's men braced themselves for an anticipated British crossing. Rumors spread that General Howe was waiting for the river to freeze, so his men could walk across. Many wondered if there would be an American army left to challenge them. Washington had about 2,400 continentals fit for duty, but many of these only had a few days left on their enlistments.[6] He needed to act fast to boost morale and save the army.

Battle of Trenton

Luckily for the Americans, General Howe eased the pressure when he suspended military activities and ordered his army into winter quarters. British and Hessian detachments made themselves comfortable throughout New Jersey, confident that they would finish off the rebels in the spring. Howe's decision presented General Washington with an unexpected opportunity. Hoping to catch the 1,400 man Hessian garrison at Trenton by surprise, he devised a daring attack.

On Christmas Day, Washington ordered the remnants of his army, just 2,400 men, to cook three days provisions, draw

---

[5] "Gen. Washington to John A. Washington, 18, December, 1776," *The George Washington Papers at the Library of Congress* : Online

[6] William Stryker's. *The Battles of Trenton and Princeton*, (Republished by The Old Barracks Assoc., Trenton NJ : 2001, Originally published in 1898), 113

new flints and ammunition, and prepare to march.[7] The riflemen with Washington were attached to four brigades. Over 230 riflemen of the 1st Continental Regiment, under Colonel Hand, were attached to General Roch de Fermoy's brigade. The remnants of Lieutenant Colonel Moses Rawlings Virginia and Maryland rifle battalion, about 100 strong, were assigned to General Hugh Mercer's brigade. The Pennsylvania state rifle regiment (originally commanded by Colonel Samuel Miles) had approximately 180 effective men and was attached to General Stirling's brigade. Lastly, the 1st, 3rd, 4th, 5th, and 6th Virginia Regiments all had rifle companies at Trenton. The 1st and 3rd Virginia were assigned to Stirling's brigade, and the other three regiments were brigaded under General Adam Stephen.[8] It appears that the rifle units served alongside the line troops rather than in their customary role as light troops. The fact that riflemen did not have bayonets was apparently not a consideration. Every man was needed for the attack.

Stephen's brigade was the first to cross the river. They formed a perimeter around the landing area. An officer on Washington's staff described the crossing in his diary:

> *Christmas, 6 p.m. -- ...It is fearfully cold and raw and a snow-storm setting in. The wind is northeast and beats in the faces of the men. It will be a terrible night for the soldiers who have no shoes. Some of them have tied old rags around their feet; others are barefoot, but I have not heard a man complain. They are ready to suffer any hardship and die rather than give up their liberty.*[9]

---

[7] "General Mercer to Col. Durkee, 25 December, 1776," in William Stryker's. *The Battles of Trenton and Princeton,* 362
[8] Lesser, "Return of the Army...December 22, 1776," 43
[9] Stryker, "Diary of an American Officer on Washington's Staff," 360

Nine hours later, from across the river, the same officer wrote,

Dec. 26, 3 a.m. -- *I am writing in the ferry house. The troops are all over, and the boats have gone back for the artillery. We are now three hours behind the set time.* Glover's men [from Massachusetts] *have had a hard time to force the boats through the floating ice with the snow drifting in their faces. I never have seen Washington so determined as he is now. He stands on the bank of the river, wrapped in his cloak, superintending the landing of the troops. He is calm and collected, but very determined. The storm is changing to sleet, and cuts like a knife. The last cannon is being landed, and we are ready to mount our horses.*[10]

The Americans started their march on Trenton around 4:00 a.m., four hours behind schedule.[11] The storm made the march very difficult on the men. Nevertheless, they pressed forward. Major James Wilkinson, an aide to General Washington, recorded in his memoirs that,

Their route was easily traced, as there was a little snow on the ground, which was tinged here and there with blood from the feet of the men who wore broken shoes."[12]

General Washington also noted the poor condition of his men, commenting that, "*Many of our poor soldiers are quite barefoot and ill-clad.*[13]

---

[10] Ibid.
[11] Stryker, 139
[12] Ibid. 129
[13] Ibid.

New Jersey

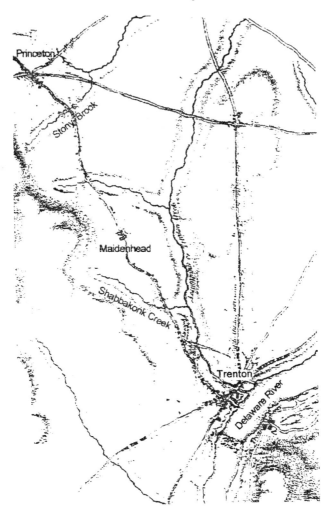

Princeton

Stony Brook

Maidenhead

Shabbakonk Creek

Trenton

Delaware River

Adapted by Lena Assad

74

About mid-way to Trenton, the column split. General Sullivan led half the men down the River Road, and General Greene took the other half along the Pennington Road. The plan called on both columns to enter Trenton simultaneously at sunrise from two directions. As dawn broke, however, they were still miles from town, and the element of surprise was in jeopardy.

Fortunately for the Americans, the same storm that delayed their march caused the Hessians to let their guard down and allowed the Americans to march to the outskirts of Trenton undetected. The first contact between the two sides occurred at the Hessian picket line, just outside Trenton, around 8:00 a.m. An aide to General Washington recorded what happened in his diary:

> *It was just 8 o'clock. Looking down the road I saw a Hessian running out from the house. He yelled in Dutch and swung his arms. Three or four others came out with their guns. Two of them fired at us, but the bullets whistled over our heads. Some of General Stephens men rushed forward and captured two.*[14]

The Americans quickly pushed the Hessian pickets into Trenton and took position of the high ground overlooking the town. Colonel Hand's riflemen moved to the left and helped secure the road to Princeton, severing that escape route. The other rifle units formed with the musket troops and prepared to storm the town, while General Henry Knox's artillery unleashed a barrage of shot.

The startled Hessians attempted to form in the streets but were harassed, first by the artillery fire and then by Washington's infantry, which pressed into town from two directions. The Hessians retreated to an apple orchard and

---

[14] Ibid. 363

desperately tried to form their lines, but the intensity of the American attack caused such confusion among the ranks that they were unable to do so. Trapped by the Assunpink Creek to their rear and the Americans on their front and flanks, the Hessians had little choice but surrender.

They suffered over a hundred casualties, including their commander, Colonel Rall, who died of his wounds the next day.[15] The Americans lost just a handful of men. Captain William Washington and Lieutenant James Monroe were both wounded in the assault, but soon recovered. With over 900 Hessian prisoners, along with much needed supplies, the attack was a staggering American success.[16] More importantly, the victory provided a huge boost to American morale.

General Washington did not want to jeopardize the victory by being caught by a British counter-attack, so he withdrew across the Delaware River. The weary American army marched back to the boats at McKonkey's Ferry, re-crossed the river, and collapsed on the other side. It had been an exhausting, yet decisive day.

News of Washington's victory quickly spread throughout the region and revived the flagging morale of Americans. While the army rested, General Washington learned that General Howe had withdrawn his troops to central New Jersey. Washington decided to fill the vacuum left by their departure. On December 30th, the American army re-crossed the river and encamped in Trenton. News of the crossing prompted General Howe to move with uncharacteristic speed. He sent approximately 8,000 men under General Cornwallis to destroy Washington's army.[17] The stage was set for round two.

---

[15] David Hackett Fischer, *Washington's Crossing*, (Oxford University Press, 2004), 405
[16] Ibid.
[17] Samuel S. Smith, *The Battle of Princeton*, (Monmouth Beach, NJ : Philip Freneau Press, 1967), 12

Princeton

General Washington expected the British to challenge him at Trenton and positioned his men along the bank of the Assunpink Creek, south of town. He concentrated his artillery on a bridge that spanned the creek. On Januray 2nd, reinforcements arrived under General John Cadwalder swelling Washington's army to approximately 6,000 men.[18]

Reports that the British were gathering in Princeton prompted General Washington to place a strong detachment along the Princeton Road to harass and retard their advance. General de Fermoy commanded these troops, which included the remnants of three Virginia regiments (the 4th, 5th and 6th Virginia Regiments), a battalion of Pennsylvania Germans, Colonel Edward Hand's 1st Continental riflemen, and six field pieces.[19]

This blocking force was posted along the Shabbakonk Creek, about three miles from Trenton. Advance parties were placed at a small creek called Five Mile Run and in the village of Maidenhead (present day Lawrenceville). When the British began their march toward Trenton at daybreak of January 2nd these American outposts were the first ones they encountered.

The American pickets at Maidenhead drew first blood when they unhorsed a jager officer who had ridden in advance of Cornwallis's vanguard. Realizing that a large enemy force was approaching, the pickets withdrew to Five Mile Run, joined the riflemen stationed there in a brief stand, and then resumed their retreat to Shabbakonk Creek.[20]

The American troops at the creek were in a bit of turmoil because their commander, General de Fermoy, had

---

[18] Samuel S. Smith, *The Battle of Princeton*, 13

[19] Dennis P Ryan, "Robert Beale Memoirs," *A Salute to Courage: The American Revolution as Seen Through Wartime Writings of Officers of the Continental Army and Navy*, (NY: Columbia University Press, 1979), 56 and Wilkinson, 135

[20] Wilkinson, 136

inexplicably abandoned them and returned to Trenton. Colonel Hand assumed command and led the first serious resistance to the British advance. His men were well concealed in a heavily forested position. The British, in contrast, advanced over mostly open terrain. Colonel Hand's men held their fire until the enemy came within point blank range and then unleashed a devastating volley that caused the British advance guard to recoil. Major James Wilkinson described the engagement:

> *The right bank of the rivulet of Shabbakon[k] was at this period covered with a close wood a mile in depth, while the opposite side presented open fields; Colonel Hand, who brought up the rear with his riflemen, determined to waste as much time as possible for the enemy at this point; he accordingly secreted his men some distance within the wood, on the flanks of the road, posting Major [Henry] Miller on the left and in person taking command of the right. In this position he waited for the flank and advanced guards of the enemy until they came within point-blank shot, and then he opened a deadly fire from his ambush, which broke and forced them back in great confusion on the main body, closely pursued by the riflemen. The boldness of this manoeuver menacing a general attack, induced the enemy to form in order of battle and bring up his artillery and open a battery, with which he scoured the wood for half an hour before he entered it.*[21]

Such determined resistance was exactly what General Washington desired because it cost Cornwallis precious daylight. Major Wilkinson noted,

---

[21] Wilkinson, 137

*This operation, [at the Shabbakonk] consumed two
hours, during which time the rifle corps took breadth
and were ready to renew the attack.*[22]

Colonel Hand's men slowly withdrew, resisting all the way
to Trenton, bringing Cornwallis's advance to a crawl. When
they passed a ravine on the outskirts of town, they joined
Colonel Scott's Virginians in another stand. With about two
hours of daylight remaining General Washington arrived on
the scene. Wilkinson recalled,

*General Washington...feeling how important it was
to retard the march of the enemy until
nightfall...thanked the detachment, and particularly
the artillery, for the services of the day, gave orders
for as obstinate a stand as could be made on that
ground, without hazarding the [artillery] pieces, and
retired to marshal his troops for action, behind the
Assanpink."*[23]

A thirty-minute artillery duel delayed the British, but they
eventually overwhelmed the Americans and continued their
advance. Ensign Robert Beale of Virginia recalled,

[Major Forsyth] *ordered to the right about face on
and off in order. We had not taken more than
regular steps until the word, 'Shift for yourselves,
boys, get over the bridge as quick as you can.' There
was running followed by a tremendous fire from the
British.*[24]

The Americans raced through town and across the Assunpick
Bridge and waited with the rest of Washington's troops for
Cornwallis to strike.

---

[22] Ibid.
[23] Ibid. 138
[24] Ryan (Robert Beale Memoirs), 56

The gravity of the moment weighed heavy on everyone. Ensign Beale recalled,

> *This was a most awful crisis. No possible chance of crossing the river; ice as large as houses floating down, and no retreat to the mountains, the British between us and them. Our brigade, consisting of the Fourth, Fifth, and Sixth Virginia Regiments, was ordered to form in column at the bridge and General Washington came and, in the presence of us all, told Colonel Scott to defend the bridge to the last extremity. Colonel Scott answered with an oath, 'Yes, General, as long as there is a man alive.'*[25]

Major Wilkinson also noted the urgency of the situation:

> *If ever there was a crisis in the affairs of the revolution,"* he recalled, *"this was the moment ; thirty minutes would have sufficed to bring the two armies into contact, and thirty more would have decided the combat...*[26]

Three times Hessian and British troops advanced towards the bridge, and each time a barrage of American artillery and small arms fire forced them back with heavy losses. The Americans would not budge, and with the last rays of daylight fading in the west General Cornwallis decided to suspend the attack and resume it in the morning. General Washington and his men had earned a twelve hour reprieve, and they made full use of it.

Around midnight, after a few hours of tense rest, most of the American army quietly withdrew from the lines and marched along a little used back road towards Princeton.

---

[25] Ryan, (Robert Beale Memoirs), 56
[26] Wilkinson, 138

Washington hoped to surprise the small British garrison there with a dawn attack. The maneuver required stealth and deception, so the men were ordered to keep silent. About 400 area militia remained in the lines at Trenton to maintain the appearance of an army preparing for battle.[27] They kept the campfires burning and continued to dig earthworks to convince the British that Washington was still there. Major Wilkinson reported that General Washington

> *Ordered the guards to be doubled, a strong fatigue party to be set to work on an intrenchment...within hearing of the sentinels of the enemy, the baggage to be sent to Burlington, the troops to be silently filed off by detachments, and the neighboring fences to be used for fuel to our guards, to keep up blazing until toward day when they had orders to retire. The night, although cloudless, was exceedingly dark, and, though calm, most severely cold, and the movement was so cautiously conducted as to elude the vigilence of the enemy.[28]*

For the most part the ruse worked. Only a handful of British sentries reported movement in the American camp, but these reports went unheeded.

The route the Americans took to Princeton barely qualified as a road and was very difficult on the horses and men. One soldier recalled,

> *The horses attached to our cannon were without shoes, and when passing over the ice they would slide in every direction, and could advance only by the assistance of the soldiers. Our men too, were without shoes or other comfortable clothing; and as traces of*

---

[27] Stryker, 275
[28] Wilkinson, 140

our march towards Princeton, the ground was literally marked with the blood of the soldiers feet.[29]

As the Americans approached the outskirts of Princeton, General Washington split his force. General Greene was sent to the left to secure a bridge at Stony Brook and enter Princeton along the Post Road, while General Sullivan continued along the back road with the bulk of the army. General Greene's column consisted of a brigade under General Hugh Mercer (between 300-350 men) and a much larger brigade under General Cadawalder (approximately 1,150). [30] Mercer's brigade included riflemen from Colonel Rawlings's Virginia/Maryland Rifle Regiment, Colonel Miles's Pennsylvania Rifle Regiment, a handful of Virginia and Delaware continentals, and the remnants of the 1st Maryland Regiment.[31]

At almost the same moment that Washington divided his army, a British column about a mile to the west crossed the Stony Brook Bridge and ascended a hill on their way to Trenton. They were reinforcements (over 400) from the 17th and 55th British Regiments under Lieutenant Colonel Charles Mawhood.[32] As they climbed the hill, some of Mawhood's horsemen caught a glimpse of Sullivan's column moving towards Princeton. Mawhood could not determine the size of the American force, but realized that the lone British regiment left in Princeton, the 40th, was in danger, so he reversed

---

[29] Sergeant R, "The Battle of Princeton," *The Pennsylvania Magazine of History and Biography, Vol. 20, No. 1* (1896), 515
[30] Wilkinson, 141, See also:
Caesar Rodney, *The Diary of Captain Thomas Rodney, 1776-1777,* (Wilmington: The Historical Society of Delaware, 1888), 33
David Hackett Fischer, *Washington's Crossing* 408 and
Samuel Smith, 34
[31] Fischer, 408
[32] Smith, 19
Note: Fischer contends that the Mawhood's column was closer to 700 men, 329

direction and rapidly marched back to town. General Washington, who was with Sullivan, soon learned about Mawhood's column. He assumed that it was only a British reconnaissance force from Princeton and ordered General Mercer to pursue and attack it before it warned the town's garrison.[33] Mercer responded quickly; he marched his brigade up a hill to the right and attempted to head off the British.[34]

Initially, Colonel Mawhood was not aware of General Mercer's troops; his concern was with Sullivan's. Major Wilkinson recalled,

> *When Colonel Mawhood...discovered the head of* [Sullivan's] *column he did not perceive General Mercer, who was marching up the creek near its left bank, and taking us* [Sullivan's column] *for a light party, as the ground concealed our numbers, he determined to retrograde and cut us up; nor had General Mercer any suspicion of the proximity of Mawhood's corps, until he recrossed Stoney brook, when a mutual discovery was made at less than 500 yards distance, and the respective corps then endeavoured to get possession of the high ground on their right.[35]*

Prior to discovering Mercer's brigade, Mawhood ordered the bulk of the 55th Regiment, which was in the rear of his column, to rejoin the 40th Regiment in Princeton. Mawhood led his remaining force, about 300 men, against Mercer. General Mercer's men collided with Mawhood's advance party in William Clark's orchard. A soldier in Mercer's detachment, known to history only as Sergeant R, described what happened:

---

[33] Smith, 20
[34] Ibid.
[35] Wilkinson, 142

As we were descending a hill through an orchard, a party of the enemy who were entrenched behind a bank and fence, rose and fired upon us. Their first shot passed over our heads cutting the limbs of the trees under which we were marching. At this moment we were ordered to wheel...We formed, advanced and fired upon the enemy. They retreated eight rods to their packs, which were laid in a line. I advanced to the fence of the opposite side of the ditch which the enemy had just left, fell on one knee and loaded my musket with ball and buckshot. Our fire was destructive; their ranks grew thin and the victory seemed nearly complete, when the British were reinforced.[36]

Mercer's men had pushed Mawhood's dismounted dragoons rearward, but now they faced Mawhood's whole force. Lieutenant James McMichael of the Pennsylvania riflemen battalion recalled the encounter:

Gen. Mercer, with 100 Pennsylvania riflemen and 20 Virginians, was detached to the front to bring on the attack. The enemy then consisting of 500 [actually closer to 300] *paraded in an open field in battle array. We boldly marched to within 25 yards of them, and then commenced the attack, which was very hot. We kept up an incessant fire until it came to pushing bayonets, when we were ordered to retreat.*[37]

Despite being reinforced by the rest of his brigade, many of Mercer's men lacked bayonets and gave way. Sergeant R noted,

---

[36] Sergeant R, 517
[37] McMichael, 141

*Many of our brave men had fallen, and we were
unable to withstand such superior numbers of fresh
troops. I soon heard General Mercer command in a
tone of distress, 'Retreat'!* [38]

Mercer's men broke and fled to the rear. They abandoned two
cannon and their commander, who was struck down and
mortally wounded by British bayonets.

Help soon arrived for Mercer's scattered troops in the form
of General Cadwalader's militiamen and a two cannon battery
under Captain William Moulder. Charles Wilson Peale served
in Cadwalader's militia and recalled,

*We marched on quickly, and met some of the troops
retreating in confusion. We continued our march
towards the hill where the firing was, though now
rather irregularly. I carried my platoon to the top of
the hill, and fired, though unwillingly, for I thought
the enemy too far off, and then retreated, loading.
We returned to the charge, and fired a second time,
and retreated as before.* [39]

Captain Thomas Rodney of Delaware also fought in General
Cadwalder's brigade and remembered that their appearance on
the field momentarily checked the British advance:

*Gen. Cadwalder's Philadelphia Brigade came up and
the enemy checked by their appearance took post
behind a fence and a ditch in front of* [William
Clark's farm] *buildings...and so extended themselves
that every man could load and fire incessantly.* [40]

---

[38] Sergeant R, 517
[39] Charles Wilson Peale, 281
[40] Rodney, *Diary of Captain Thomas Rodney*, 34

With British cannon and musketry pouring in on them, Cadwalader's inexperienced troops grew jumpy. Yet, according to Captain Rodney, "*Gen. Cadwalader led up the head of the column with the greatest bravery to within 50 yards of the enemy.*"[41] This was too much for many of Cadwalder's men. Captain Rodney noted that the advance,

> *Was rashly done, for* [Cadwalder] *was obliged to recoil; and leaving one piece of his artillery, he fell back 40 yards and endeavored to form the brigade, and some companies did form and gave a few vollies but the fire of the enemy was so hot, that, at the sight of troops running to the rear, the militia gave way and the whole brigade broke and most of them retired to a woods about 150 yards in the rear, but two pieces of artillery stood their ground and were served with great skill and bravery.*[42]

The battery that held its ground was commanded by Captain Joseph Moulder, and for a few minutes his two cannon, along with a handful of intrepid infantry, were the only American presence on the battlefield. Captain Rodney commanded a portion of the infantry and recalled,

> *We...took position behind some stacks just to the left of the artillery; and about 30 of the Philadelphia Infantry were under cover of a house on our left and a little in the rear. About 15 of my men came to this post, but I could not keep them all there, for the enemies fire was dreadful....From these stacks and buildings we, with the two pieces of artillery kept up a continuous fire on the enemy; and in all probability it was this circumstance that prevented the enemy*

[41] Rodney, 34-35
[42] Ibid. 35

from advancing, for they could not tell the number we had posted behind these covers and were afraid to attempt passing them; but if they had known how few there were they might easily have advanced while the two brigades were in confusion and routed the whole body for it was a long time before they could be reorganized again, and indeed many, that were panic struck, ran quite off.[43]

The determined stand of Moulder, Rodney, and their men not only allowed Cadwalder's and Mercer's brigades to reform, but also allowed reinforcements to take a strong position on the battlefield. These reinforcements, continentals from New England and Virginia as well as Colonel Edward Hand's Pennsylvania riflemen, rushed to the fight from General Sullivan's column. They were accompanied by General Washington who strenuously rallied Cadwalader's and Mercer's men. Sergeant R observed Washington's efforts:

Washington appeared in front of the American army, riding towards those of us who were retreating, and exclaimed 'Parade with us, my brave fellows, there is but a handful of the enemy, and we will have them directly'[44]

The effect of his appeal was electric. Sergeant R recalled, "*I immediately joined the main body, and marched over the ground again.*"[45] Washington led the restored American line, which significantly outflanked the British, towards Mawhood's troops. The British momentarily stood firm and then began an orderly retreat. When Colonel Hand's riflemen moved against their left flank, the British retreat turned into a

---

[43] Rodney, 35-36
[44] Sergeant R, 517
[45] Ibid.

rout.   Major Wilkinson noted that, *"the riflemen were...the first in pursuit, and in fact took the greatest part of the prisoners."* [46] They were urged on by General Washington who gleefully exclaimed, *"It's a fine fox chase, boys!"* [47]

Most of the fleeing British took a circular route to Trenton, but some withdrew towards Princeton where they found General Sullivan's column pushing the 40th and 55th Regiments. Many of the fugitives sought shelter in Nassau Hall, a large brick building in town. A blast of artillery quickly convinced them to surrender, however, and Washington's victory was complete. At the cost of less than forty men killed, including General Mercer who died of his wounds a few days later, and another forty wounded, the Americans inflicted a second stunning defeat on General Howe's army. British losses in killed, wounded, and captured numbered between 400 to 500 men. [48]

General Washington was tempted to stage one more daring act, an assault on the vital supply depot at New Brunswick. He decided against it, however, because his men were exhausted and in no condition to face Cornwallis, who was rapidly marching eastward from Trenton. Reluctantly, Washington headed north, towards Morristown, and the safety of New Jersey's mountains.

---

[46] Wilkinson, 145

[47] Ibid.

[48] Fischer, 414-415

Note: General Mercer died of his wounds a few days after the battle.

Morristown Encampment

As was the custom of the time, both armies suspended the campaign and settled into winter quarters. Washington encamped near Morristown, New Jersey, and used the Watchtung Mountains as a defensive barrier. He hoped to maintain the American army until reinforcements arrived in the spring. To combat one of the scourges of both armies, General Washington ordered smallpox inoculations for his men. This month long process left the Americans very vulnerable to attack. Fortunately, General Howe did not press the Americans, and the inoculations were successfully completed.

Significant reinforcements arrived at Morristown in the spring, swelling the American army's ranks to over 8,000 men.[49] Virginia sent six new regiments, (the 10th through 15th Regiments). One of them, the 11th Virginia, differed from all the other Virginia regiments in that it had more riflemen than musket-men. Colonel Daniel Morgan commanded this special unit. He returned to Virginia in the fall of 1776, after eight months of captivity in Quebec, and helped recruit his new regiment.[50]

---

[49] "General Washington to Congress, 21 May, 1777," *The Papers of George Washington* (Library of Congress Online)

[50] Note: There has long been a misunderstanding about the make up of the 11th Virginia Regiment. Virginia regiments raised a year earlier consisted of seven musket and three rifle companies. Five of the six new regiments were organized in similar fashion. The 11th Virginia was different, however. Half of the regiment (five of its ten companies) consisted of the independent rifle companies raised in the state during the summer of 1776. Only one of these rifle company remained intact after the fall of Fort Washington. It was commanded by Captain William Blackwell of Fauquier County. Captain Blackwell's first lieutenant was twenty year old John Marshall, future Chief Justice of the Supreme Court. The other half of the 11th Virginia consisted of three musket companies from northern Virginia and two rifle companies from Frederick County. Two other rifle

More riflemen joined Washington's ranks through an independent corps commanded by Major Mynheer Ottendorf of France. The unit originally consisted of 60 light infantry and two 45 man rifle companies.[51] Captain John Paul Schott and Antonie Selin commanded these riflemen. They joined

---

companies, one from Pennsylvania and the other from Virginia, were added to the regiment after it arrived in New Jersey

There are a number of points that support the contention that the 11th Virginia included musket companies. First, the 11th Virginia was never referred to, in contemporary sources, as a rifle regiment. In fact, at least two pension applications from members of the 11th Virginia, refer to the unit as, "*Morgan's musket regiment.*" In 1818 Eden Clevenger, a former rifleman in Captain Porterfield's company, claimed in a pension application that he served, "*in the 11th Virginia Regiment, generally called Col. Morgan's musket regiment.*" His claim was supported by Thomas Stothard, who declared that, "*he went out with Eden Clevenger in the regiment of musket men in the same company and messed with him all the time of service.*"

The fact that some of Morgan's men marched north unarmed, and were supplied with weapons (probably muskets) when they arrived in camp, also supports the view that there were musket-men in the 11th Virginia. Lastly, when a special rifle corps was actually formed, in June, 1777, most members of the 11th Virginia remained with the regiment. And many of the riflemen who stayed had to exchange their rifles for muskets, per order of General Washington.

See: H.R. McIlwaine, ed. *Journals of the Council of the State of Virginia, Vol. 1,* (Richmond : Virginia State Library, 1931), 325 ;
E.M. Sanchex-Saavedra, *A Guide to Virginia Military Organizations in the American Revolution, 1774-1787,* (Westminster, MD : Willow Bend, 1978), 65 ;
John Cullen, *The Papers of John Marshall, Vol. 1,* (University of North Carolina Press, 1977),
W.T.R. Saffell, *Records of the Revolutionary War, 3rd Ed.,* (Baltimore: Charles Saffell, 1894), 256-268

[51] Journal of Continental Congress, 5 December, 1776 (Accessed thru the Library of Congress, Online)

the army in the spring and engaged in a number of skirmishes with General Howe's advance troops.

The influx of reinforcements prompted Washington to restructure the army. In May, he formed new brigades, and in June, he ordered the formation of a corps of riflemen.

Morgan's Rifle Corps

Although General Washington was encouraged by the number of men who joined his ranks in 1777, he still had a few glaring shortfalls to address. One was the need for an effective body of light infantry. The British used their light infantry as flankers and skirmishers. They often combined these soldiers with German Jagers (riflemen) and British dragoons for reconnaissance activities.

General Washington largely relied on militia troops for such duty in 1776 and found them ineffective. Washington's orders for June 1st, 1777, suggest that he had settled on a replacement for the militia:

The commanding officer of every Corps is to make a report early to morrow morning...of the number of Rifle-men under his command—In doing which, he is to include none but such as are known to be perfectly skilled in the use of these guns, and who are known to be active and orderly in their behaviour. [52]

Two weeks later, on June 13th, Washington formed a new rifle corps and appointed Colonel Daniel Morgan to its command. Washington informed Colonel Morgan that,

---

[52] "General Orders, 1 June, 1777," *The Papers of George Washington, Vol. 9,* 578

The corps of Rangers newly formed and under your command, are to be considered as a body of light infantry, and are to act as such, for which reason they will be exempted from the common duties of the line.[53]

An apparent shortage of rifles caused Washington to order,

Such rifles as belong to the States, in the different brigades, to be immediately exchanged with Col. Morgan for musquets...If a sufficient number of rifles (public property) can not be procured, the Brigadiers are requested to assist Col. Morgan, either by exchanging, or purchasing those that are private property.[54]

General Washington also made arrangements for the riflemen to receive spears as a defense against mounted troops. He informed Colonel Morgan that,

I have sent for Spears, which I expect shortly to receive and deliver you, as a defence against Horse; till you are furnished with these, take care not to be caught in such a Situation as to give them any advantage over you.[55]

The spears arrived a week later. General Washington was pleased, but recommended a few adjustments to suit the riflemen:

---

[53] "General Washington to Colonel Morgan, 13 June, 1777," *The Papers of George Washington*: Vol. 10, 31

[54] "General Orders, 13 June, 1777," *The Papers of George Washington*: Vol. 10, 20

[55] "General Washington to Colonel Morgan, 13 June, 1777," *The Papers of George Washington*: Vol. 10, 31

The Spears have come to hand, and are very handy and will be useful to the Rifle Men. But they would be more conveniently carried, if they had a sling fixed to them, they should also have a spike in the but end to fix them in the ground and they would then serve as a rest for the Rifle. The Iron plates which fix the spear head to the shaft, should be at least eighteen inches long to prevent the Shaft from being cut through, with a stroke of a Horseman's Sword.[56]

It is unclear how long the riflemen actually used the spears. No further reference to them appears after June 20th, which suggests the cumbersome weapons were quickly discarded by the riflemen.

Morgan's corps comprised riflemen from Virginia and Pennsylvania (500 in all), and the unit was immediately put to use. On the day of its formation, General Washington ordered Colonel Morgan to

Take post at Van Vechten's Bridge, and watch, with very small scouting parties (to avoid fatiguing your men too much...) the enemy's left flank...In case of any movement of the enemy, you are instantly to fall upon their flanks, and gall them as much as possible, taking especial care not to be surrounded, or to have your retreat to the army cut off.[57]

The next day, General Howe sent a large detachment towards the American lines. Washington sent the rifle corps forward to skirmish with them. He described the engagement in a letter to General Sullivan:

---

[56] General Washington to Richard Peters, 20 June, 1777," *The Papers of George Washington*: Vol. 10, 88

[57] "General Washington to Colonel Morgan, 13 June, 1777," *The Papers of George Washington*: Vol. 10, 31

The Enemy have advanced a party; said to be two thousand, as far as Van Ests Mill upon Millstone River. They have been skirmishing with Colo. Morgans Riflemen but have halted on a piece of high ground.[58]

Two days later Washington reiterated his orders to Colonel Morgan:

You will continue to keep out your active parties carefully watching every motion of the enemy; and have your whole body in readiness to move without confusion, and free from danger....[59]

The British held their position for nearly a week and skirmished daily with Morgan's riflemen. When Howe finally withdrew, Morgan's rifle corps pursued them all the way to Piscataway. Washington noted that, *"In the pursuit, Colo. Morgans Rifle Men exchanged several sharp Fires with the Enemy, which it is imagined did them considerable execution."* [60] Captain Thomas Posey of Virginia commanded one of Morgan's rifle companies and provided a detailed account of the engagement in his biography:

The [rifle] regiment was posted in a thick wood somewhat swampy near the rode, & when the main body of the enemy passed, & the rear guard came on, Morgan ordered the regiment to attack and indeavour to cut it off. The order was promptly obeyed, & the action was warmly contested on both

---

[58] "General Washington to General Sullivan, 14 June, 1777," *The Papers of George Washington, Vol. 10,* 40
[59] "Richard Meade to Daniel Morgan, 16 June, 1777," *The Papers of George Washington, Vol. 10,* 40
[60] "General Washington to John Hancock, 22 June, 1777," *The Papers of George Washington, Vol. 10,* 104-105

sides; in the course of the action Capt. Posey was ordered with his company across a causeway, being through a considerable swamp to gain the front of the enemy which was promptly executed & a sharp conflict took place, but the light Infantry of the enemy surrounded his company, and was near cutting him off [when] *he, perceiving his situation, ordered a well directed fire upon a particular part of the enemy, which opened a passage for him to retreat through. Through the course of the action the regiment sustained considerable loss in killed & wounded, the enemy suffered very considerably, tho' the highest loss fell upon Capt. Posey's company.*[61]

General Washington believed that his rifle corps had soundly thrashed the enemy:

I fancy the British Grenadiers got a pretty severe peppering yesterday by Morgan's Riffle Corp – they fought it seems a considerable time within the distance of, from twenty to forty yards...more than a hundd of them must have fallen.[62]

Four days later, General Howe renewed his efforts to draw Washington out of his fortified lines with a sudden march towards the American left flank. This movement surprised the Americans and was nearly a disaster for the rifle corps. Captain John Chilton of the 3rd Virginia Regiment, described what happened:

---

[61] *"A Short Biography of the Life of Governor Thomas Posey,"* Thomas Posey Papers, Indiana Historical Society Library, Indianapolis, IN (Referred to henceforth as Posey's Biography)
[62] "General Washington to Joseph Reed, 23 June, 1777," *The Papers of George Washington, Vol. 10,* 115

Col. Morgan with the Rifle Regmt. was on the Mattuchin lines at the time and our main army had come down into the Plains. The Enemy unexpectedly stole a march in the night of the 25th and had nearly surrounded Morgan before he was aware of it. He with difficulty saved his men and baggage and after a retreat, rallied his men and sustained a heavy charge until reinforced by Major Genl. Ld. Stirling, who gave them so warm a reception that they were obliged to retreat so precipitately that it had like to have become a rout. But being strongly reinforced he [Stirling] was obliged to retreat with the loss of 2 pieces of Artillery.[63]

Morgan's riflemen were not the only ones heavily engaged with the British. Ottendorf's independent corps was nearly decimated in a rear guard action in late June. Lieutenant Colonel Charles Armand, who replaced Ottendorf in May after Ottendorf suddenly left the army, reported that he lost 32 men out of 80 engaged.[64] William Grant, a Virginia rifleman, witnessed the action and noted that Armand's men

Drew up immediately in order to defend their field pieces and cover our retreat, and in less than an hour and a half were entirely cut off; Scarce sixty of them returned safe out of the field; those who did escape were so scattered over the country that a great

---

[63] Lyon Tyler, "John Chilton to his brother, 29 June, 1777", *Tyler's Quarterly Historical and Genealogical Magazine, Vol. 12,* (Richmond, VA: Richmond Press Inc., 1931), 118

[64] See: Jim Filipski and Steve Collward, *A Chronology of the Appointments & Commands of Captain Antooni Selin and His Association with the Independent Corps of Captain John Paul Schott, Major Nicholas de Ottendorf and Col. Charles Armand,*
(accessed at www.captainselinscompany.org/chronology.html)

number of them could not rejoin the Army for five or six days.[65]

Johann Buttner, of Armand's Corps, was one of those scattered men. He recalled,

When we saw that we were outnumbered and resistance was hopeless, we abandoned our cannon and baggage and fled down the other side of the hill. Many threw away their rifles and knapsacks, and ran like hares into the forest. I fell into a ditch and my comrades, leaving me for dead, jumped over me. As the cannon balls and rifle bullets were falling all around me and I was afraid of being run through by the enemy that were pursuing us, I crawled on my hands and knees into some thick undergrowth nearby, and lay there till I could no longer hear any firing.[66]

Although American advance parties were pounded by the British and forced to retreat, the main American position remained secure. General Howe, discouraged at his failure to draw the American army away from its fortified position and into an open engagement, withdrew to New York to develop a new plan of attack.

In July, General Howe placed the bulk of his army on ships and sailed out to sea. He showed up six weeks later in the Chesapeake Bay, en route to Philadelphia via Maryland. General Washington scrambled to oppose Howe and defend the capital. He had over 10,000 men, but he lacked a very valuable asset, Daniel Morgan's Rifle Corps.[67]

---

[65] Ibid.

[66] *Narrative of Johann Carl Buettner in the American Revolution*, (NY ; Benjamin Bloom, 1971), 43-44

[67] Boatner, 109

The Rifle Corps Heads North

Prior to Howe's arrival in Chesapeake Bay, General Washington received alarming news from New York. A large British army, under General John Burgoyne, was advancing down Lake Champlain and the Hudson River Valley from Canada. Burgoyne planned to occupy Albany and sever New England from the rest of the colonies with his 7,000 many army. A thousand Indians accompanied Burgoyne and spread terror on the march.

General Philip Schuyler, the commander of American forces in New York, complained that he was powerless to resist Burgoyne's advance because fear of the Indians had infected his troops:

> *The most unaccountable panic has seized the Troops...A few shot from a small party of Indians has more than once thrown them into the greatest Confusion – The Day before Yesterday three hundred of our Men...came running in, being drove by a few Indians, certainly not more than fifty.*[68]

General Schuyler also lamented about his lack of troops:

> *We have not one Militia from the Eastern States & under forty from this – Can it therefore any longer be a matter of Surprise that we are obligated to give way and retreat before a vastly superior force daily increasing in numbers....*[69]

General Washington responded and sent Morgan's Rifle Corps north to counteract the Indians. Washington expressed his high regard for Morgan's men in his orders:

---

[68] "General Philip Schuyler to General George Washington, 1 August, 1777," *The Papers of George Washington, Vol.* 10, 482-483

[69] "General Philip Schuyler to General George Washington, 13 August, 1777," *The Papers of George Washington, Vol. 10,* 606

You will march...with [your] corps to Peekskill, taking with you all the baggage belonging to it. When you arrive there, you will take directions from General Putnam, who, I expect, will have vessels provided to carry you to Albany. The approach of the enemy in that quarter has made a further reinforcement necessary. I know of no corps so likely to check their progress, in proportion to its number, as that under your command. I have great dependence on you, your officers and men, and I am persuaded you will do honor to yourselves, and essential services to your country.[70]

Washington also expressed his confidence in the rifle corps to New York Governor George Clinton:

I am forwarding as fast as possible, to join the Northern army, Colonel Morgan's corps of riflemen, amounting to about five hundred. These are all chosen men, selected from the army at large, well acquainted with the use of rifles, and with that mode of fighting, which is necessary to make them a good counterpoise to the Indians; and they have distinguished themselves on a variety of occasions, since the formation of the corps, in skirmishes with the enemy. I expect the most eminent services from them, and I shall be mistaken if their presence does not go far towards producing a general desertion among the savages.[71]

---

[70] "General Washington to Colonel Daniel Morgan, 16 August, 1777," *The Papers of George Washington, Vol. 10,* 641
[71] "General Washington to George Clinton, 16 August, 1777," *The Papers of George Washington, Vol. 10* , 634-636

Colonel Morgan's orders were slightly adjusted during his march to New York. Congress removed General Schuyler from command of the northern army and installed General Horatio Gates in his place. Morgan was instructed to report directly to General Gates, who was encamped with the army north of Albany.

Gates was pleased to hear of the rifle corps' transfer and expressed his sentiments in a letter to General Washington:

> *I cannot sufficiently thank your Excellency for sending Colonel Morgan's corps to this army; they will be of the greatest service to it, for until the late successes this way, I am told the army were quite panic-struck by their Indians, and their Tory and Canadian assassins in Indian dresses.* [72]

The "late successes" that Gates referred to included the defense of Fort Stanwix and the stunning American victory at Bennington, where 2,000 New Hampshire and Vermont militia overwhelmed a 900 man foraging party from Burgoyne's army.[73] These victories significantly improved American morale. By September, General Gates's army surpassed Burgoyne's in size, and a new sense of optimism gripped the Americans.[74] This feeling was heightened by the arrival of Morgan's corps in September.

Morgan's unit was not at full strength when it arrived in New York. Three months of active service and the long march north took a toll on the rifle corps. Less than 400

---

[72] "General Gates to General Washington, 22 August, 1777," *The Papers of George Washington, Vol. 11*, 38

[73] Boatner, 75

[74] Charles H. Lesser, ed. "A General Return of the Continental Troops Under the Command of Major General Horatio Gates, 7 September, 1777 (Gates Papers) in *The Sinews of Independence: Monthly Strength Reports of the Continental Army*, (Chicago: The Univ. of Chicago Press, 1976), 49

riflemen arrived with Colonel Morgan.[75] General Gates partially alleviated Morgan's manpower shortage by drafting fifteen of the most hardy musket-men from each regiment to serve in a light infantry corps.[76] They were led by Major Henry Dearborn of New Hampshire and attached to Colonel Morgan's command. The addition of 250 hand-picked musket-men with bayonets greatly enhanced the fighting capabilities of Morgan's corps. They would soon have the opportunity to demonstrate their capabilities on the battlefields of Saratoga.

---

[75] General James Wilkinson, "A Return of Colonel Morgan's detachment of Riflemen, 3 September, 1777," *Memoirs of My Own Times, Vol. 1* (Philadelphia: Abraham Small, 1816) Appendix C Reprinted by AMS Press Inc., :NY, 1973

[76] Graham, "General Gates to Colonel Morgan, 29 August, 1777," *The Life of General Daniel Morgan,* 138

Chapter Five

Saratoga

With a counter measure to Burgoyne's Indians finally in camp and an influx of reinforcements swelling his ranks, General Gates advanced north with his army. On September 12th, they arrived at Bemis Heights, an excellent defensive position overlooking the Hudson River, and waited for the British, who slowly approached from the north. By September 15th, General Burgoyne's army was just a few miles from Bemis Heights. Burgoyne knew that a large American force lay to his front, but he was unsure of its strength and placement. Undeterred by uncertainty, Burgoyne boldly advanced towards the Americans on September 19th.[1]

Battle of Freeman's Farm

General Burgoyne divided his army into three columns. The left column, commanded by General von Riesdel, comprised approximately 1,600 men.[2] It included most of the artillery and a large baggage train protected by the 47th British regiment. The column slowly marched along the river road towards the Americans at Bemis Heights. General Burgoyne's right column, commanded by General Simon Fraser, was his largest detachment with 2,400 men.[3] Fraser's task was to screen the army's right flank while probing the American left.

---

[1] James Baxter, ed., *The British Invasion from the North: Digby's Journal of the Campaigned of Generals Carleton and Burgoyne from Canada, 1776-1777*, (New York : De Capa Press, 1970), 267
[2] John Luzader, *Decision on the Hudson: The Battles of Saratoga*, (Eastern National, 2002), 41
[3] Ibid.

To do this, Fraser marched nearly three miles west, away from the river, and then swung south towards the Americans.

General Burgoyne marched with the center column in a diagonal direction from the river. The column totaled 1,500 men from the 9th, 20th, 21st, and 62nd British regiments and was commanded by General James Hamilton. Four pieces of artillery were also part of this column.[4]

The three columns began their march around 9:00 a.m. and were immediately spotted by American pickets. Word reached the American camp that the enemy was on the move. Colonel James Wilkinson, an aide to General Gates, recalled that General Gates,

> *Ordered Colonel Morgan to advance his corps, who was instructed, should he find the enemy approaching, to hang on their front and flanks, to retard their march, and cripple them as much as possible.* [5]

Morgan's light corps, numbering around 600 men, advanced through the thick woods in two sections.[6] They marched about a mile and a half and emerged onto the edge of an abandoned farm. The clearing was dotted with trees and stumps. Two small buildings, described as cabins by many eyewitnesses, sat on a rise of ground about 300 yards away. The opposite wood line was only 150 yards beyond the cabins.

---

[4] Richard M. Ketchum, *Saratoga,: Turning Point of America's Revolutionary War*, (NY: Holt & Co., 1997), 357

[5] General James Wilkinson, *Memoirs of My Own Times, Vol. 1*, (Philadelphia: Abraham Small, 1816, Reprinted by AMS Press Inc., 1973), 236

[6] Wilkinson, Appendix E and Joseph Lee Boyle, "From Saratoga to Valley Forge: The Diary of Lt. Samuel Armstrong," *The Pennsylvania Magazine of History and Biography,* Vol. 121 No. 3 (July 1997), 245 (Henceforth referred to as Lieutenant Armstrong's Diary)

Freeman Farm

Adapted by Lena Assad

Morgan's corps arrived at the clearing just as an enemy advance party attacked the American picquet guard posted in the cabins. Samuel Armstrong, a member of Major Dearborn's light infantry, described the encounter:

> [At] *about 12 Oclock we were Alarm'd by the firing of two or three Musketts from the Enemies Scouts, upon which the Riffle and Light Infantry Battalions were Ordered off to Scour the Woods. We forwarded down to our Picquet Guard where we had no sooner got Sight of than we saw the Enemy surrounding them.* [7]

The American pickets quickly dispersed and fled Freeman's Farm in the face of the approaching enemy. [8] As the British skirmishers pushed past the cabins and neared the southern wood line, however, they collided with the bulk of Morgan's light corps. British Lieutenant William Digby described what happened:

> *A little after 12 our advanced picquets came up with Colonel Morgan and engaged, but from the great superiority of fire received from him – his numbers being much greater – they were obliged to fall back, every officer being either killed or wounded except one.* [9]

The British skirmishers, outnumbered and outgunned, retreated under a deadly barrage of fire. Advance elements of

---

[7] Lieutenant Armstrong's Diary, 245

[8] Earl of Harrington in, John Burgoyne, *A State of the Expedition from Canada*, (New York Times & Arno Press, 1969), 68
Note: This account is supported by the observation of American Lieutenant Colonel James Wilkinson, who saw British bodies lying around the cabins after the initial engagement, but prior to the resumption of battle.

[9] Digby Journal, 272

Morgan's corps pursued them across the field and into the woods beyond. The pursuit abruptly ended when the Americans encountered British reinforcements. These soldiers, eager to fire on the Americans, did so without orders and before all of their comrades from the advance party had cleared their front.[10] The result was more loss for the battered British skirmishers and an end to the American pursuit.

Morgan's corps, which was already disorganized by the charge, disintegrated in retreat. Men ran in all directions to escape the enemy. The sudden emergence of two British companies and a cannon from General Fraser's column added urgency to their flight.[11]

Appalled by the turn of events, Colonel Morgan struggled to reorganize his shattered corps. He used an uncommon military tool to do so, a turkey whistle. Colonel Wilkinson, appeared on the scene soon after the fight and observed Morgan's efforts to reform his riflemen:

My ears were saluted by an uncommon noise, which I approached, and perceived Colonel Morgan attended by two men only, who with a turkey call was collecting his dispersed troops. The moment I came up to him, he burst into tears, and exclaimed, 'I am ruined, by G—d! Major Morris ran on so rapidly with the front, that they were beaten before I could get up with the rear, and my men are scattered God knows where.' I remarked to the Colonel that he had a long day before him to retrieve an inauspicious beginning, and informed him where I had seen his field officers, which appeared to cheer him....[12]

---

[10] Horatio Rogers ed., *Hadden's Journal and Orderly Book: A Journal Kept in Canada and Upon Burgoyne's Campaign in 1776 and 1777,* (Boston: Gregg Press, 1972), 163
(Henceforth referred to as Hadden Journal)
[11] Anburey, 172
[12] Wilkinson, 238

One of the field officers that Colonel Wilkinson met prior to Morgan was Major Joseph Morris. Morris led the charge against the fleeing British pickets and gave Wilkinson a detailed account of the engagement:

> *From him* [Major Morris] *I learnt that the corps was advancing by files in two lines, when they unexpectedly fell upon a picket of the enemy, which they almost instantly forced, and pursuing the fugitives, their front had as unexpectedly fallen in with the British line; that several officers and men had been made prisoners, and that to save himself, he had been obliged to push his horse through the ranks of the enemy, and escaped by a circuitous route.* [13]

Wilkinson also encountered Lieutenant Colonel Richard Butler, the rifle corps' second in command. He confirmed Morris's account:

> *I* [Wilkinson] *crossed the angle of the field, leapt the fence, and just before me on a ridge discovered Lieutenant-colonel Butler with three men, all tree'd; from him I learnt that they had 'caught a Scotch prize,' that having forced the picket, they had closed with the British line, had been instantly routed, and from the suddenness of the shock and the nature of the ground, were broken and scattered in all directions.* [14]

Thanks to a pause in the conflict, Colonel Morgan was able to reorganize his riflemen. They formed in the woods on the extreme right of the American line. [15] A marshy ravine

---

[13] Ibid. 237
[14] Ibid.
[15] Hadden Journal, 164

protected their right flank. To their left, fresh American troops from the brigades of General Poor and General Learned extended the line westward. Major Dearborn's light infantry formed on the left of the American line and were separated from the riflemen for the rest of the day.

The battle resumed around mid afternoon when General Hamilton's center column emerged from the far woods and advanced upon the Americans. They concentrated on a small ridge just beyond the Freeman house. Lieutenant James Hadden, a British artillery officer, described the action:

> *The Enemy being in possession of the wood almost immediately attacked the Corps which took post beyond two log Huts on Freemans Farm...I was advanced with two Guns to the left of the 62nd Regt and ye two left companies being formed en potence* [refused or bent to protect the flank] *I took post in the Angle...In this situation we sustained a heavy tho intermitting fire from near three hours....*[16]

The American fire, enhanced by the accuracy of the riflemen, was especially hard on the British artillerymen. Lieutenant Hadden lost 19 out of 22 men and all of his horses. The 62nd regiment lost nearly half of its men. [17]

Hadden's position was not the only hot spot, however. The battle raged all along the line. British Lieutenant William Digby noted that he had never seen anything like it:

> *Such an explosion of fire I never had any idea of before, and the heavy artillery joining in concert like great peals of thunder, assisted by the echoes of the woods, almost deafened us with the noise.* [18]

---

[16] Ibid. 165
[17] Ibid.
[18] Digby Journal, 237

British corporal Roger Lamb gave a similar account:

The conflict was dreadful; for four hours a constant blaze of fire was kept up, and both armies seemed to be determined on death or victory...Men, and particularly officers, dropped every moment on each side. Several of the Americans placed themselves in high trees, and as often as they could distinguish a British officer's uniform, took him off by deliberately aiming at his person.[19]

The impact of American markmenship was also noted by Colonel James Wilkinson, who observed that it repeatedly drove the British from the Freeman house hill:

The fire of our marksmen from this wood was too deadly to be withstood by the enemy in line, and when they gave way and broke, our men rushing from their cover, pursued them to the eminence, where having their flanks protected, they [the enemy] rallied and charging in turn drove us back into the wood, from whence a dreadful fire would again force them to fall back; and in this manner did the battle fluctuate, like waves of a stormy sea, with alternate advantage for four hours without one moment's intermission. The British artillery fell into our possession at every charge, but we could neither turn the pieces upon the enemy, nor bring them off...The slaughter of this brigade of artillerists was remarkable, the captain and thirty-six men being killed or wounded out of forty-eight.[20]

[19] Roger Lamb, *An Original and Authentic Journal of Occurrences During the Late American War from Its Commencement to 1783*, (Dublin: Wilkinson & Courtney, 1809), 159
Reprinted by Arno Press, 1968
[20] Wilkinson, 241

Even General Burgoyne acknowledged the impact of the riflemen:

> *The enemy had with their army great numbers of marksmen, armed with rifle-barrel pieces; these during an engagement, hovered upon the flanks in small detachments, and were very expert in securing themselves, and in shifting their ground. In this action many placed themselves in high trees in the rear of their own line, and there was seldom a minute's interval of smoke, in any part of our line without officers being taken off by single shot. It will naturally be supposed, that the Indians would be of great use against this mode of fighting. The example of those that remained after the great desertion proved the contrary, for not a man of them was to be brought within the sound of a rifle shot.* [21]

As sunset approached, the British were in serious trouble. The 62nd regiment was shattered, and the other regiments were barely holding on. Suddenly, drums were heard in the woods beyond the American right flank. German reinforcements, under General Riedesel, emerged from the forest and onto the field to relieve the British. They slammed into the right flank of the startled Americans. A German artillery officer, Captain Pausch, recalled,

> *I had shells brought up and placed by the side of the cannon and as soon as I got the range, I fired twelve or fourteen shots in quick succession into the foe who were within good pistol shot distance.* [22]

---

[21] Burgoyne, 39-40

[22] George Pausch, *Journal of Captain Pausch, Chief of the Hanau Artillery During the Burgoyne Campaign*, Translated by William L. Stone, (Albany, NY: Joel Munsell's Sons, 1886), 137-138

The arrival of the Germans revived British spirits, and they rallied one more time. Captain Pausch noted,

> *The firing from muskets was at once renewed, and assumed lively proportions, particularly the platoon fire from the left wing of Riedesel. Presently, the enemy's fire, though very lively at one time, suddenly ceased. I advanced about sixty paces sending a few shells after the flying enemy, and firing from twelve to fifteen shots more into the woods into which they had retreated. Everything then became quiet; and about fifteen minutes afterwards darkness set in....* [23]

One of the most intense battles of the Revolutionary War was over, and the carnage was appalling. The field was littered with dead and wounded men who remained unattended all night. Lieutenant Digby described the scene:

> *During the night we remained in our ranks, and tho we heard the groans of our wounded and dying at a small distance, yet could not assist them till morning, not knowing the position of the enemy, and expecting the action would be renewed at day break. Sleep was a stranger to us...*
> *20th. At day break we sent out parties to bring in our wounded, and lit fires as we were almost froze with cold, and our wounded who lived till the morning must have severely felt it.* [24]

British ensign Thomas Anburey had the misfortune to command a burial party the next day:

---

[23] Ibid. 138
[24] Digby, 274

The day after our late engagement, I had as unpleasant a duty as can fall to the lot of an officer, the command of the party sent out to bury the dead and bring in the wounded...They [the wounded] had remained out all night, and from the loss of blood and want of nourishment, were upon the point of expiring with faintness; some of them begged they might lie and die, others again were insensible, some upon the least movement were put in the most horrid tortures, and all had near a mile to be conveyed to the hospitals; others at their last gasp, who for want of our timely assistance must have inevitably expired. These poor creatures, perishing with cold and weltering in their blood, displayed such a scene, it must be a heart of adamant that could not be affected at it. [25]

Although the British kept the field, it was at a heavy cost; they suffered twice as many casualties as the Americans. Some of the British, like Thomas Anburey, questioned the value of the victory:

Notwithstanding the glory of the day remains on our side, I am fearful the real advantage resulting from this hard fought battle will rest on that of the Americans, our army being so weakened by this engagement as not to be of sufficient strength to venture forth and improve the victory, which may, in the end, put a stop to our intended expedition; the only apparent benefit gained is that we keep possession of the ground where the engagement began. [26]

---

[25] Anburey, 176
[26] Ibid. 175

General Burgoyne, in a letter to Lord George Germain, reached a similar conclusion about the victory:

> *It was soon found that no fruits, honour excepted, were attained by the preceding victory, the enemy working with redoubled ardour to strengthen their left, their right was already unattackable.*[27]

Despite their retreat from the field, the attitude in the American camp was far from defeatist. In fact, most American accounts bragged about punishing the enemy and attributed the retreat merely to darkness. Major Dearborn's observation was typical:

> *On this Day has Been fought one of the Greatest Battles that Ever was fought in America, & I Trust we have Convinced the British Butchers that the Cowardly yankees Can & when there is a Call for it, will, fight...The Enimy Brought almost their whole force against us, together with 8 pieces of Artilery. But we who had Something more at Stake than fighting for six Pence Pr Day kept our ground til Night Closed the scene, & then Both Parties Retire'd.*[28]

Many of the British did indeed change their opinion of the Americans after the battle. Ensign Thomas Anburey's comments were typical:

---

[27] "Burgoyne to Germaine, 10 October, 1777," *A State of the Expedition,* Appendix, 88
[28] Dearborn Journal, 106

The courage and obstinacy with which the Americans fought were the astonishment of everyone, and we now become fully convinced they are not that contemptible enemy we had hitherto imagined them, incapable of standing a regular engagement, and that they would only fight behind strong and powerful works.[29]

Colonel Morgan's riflemen were some of the combatants that Amburey referred to. They engaged the British for nearly eight hours and inflicted heavy losses on them. They, in turn, suffered only sixteen casualties, seven killed and nine wounded.[30] The extended range of rifles, which allowed Morgan's men to fire from beyond musket distance, contributed to the low rifle casualties. In contrast, Major Dearborn's light infantry battalion, armed with smoothbore muskets, had the highest number of unit deaths, with eighteen. Twenty-two others were wounded. [31] An official count of American casualties listed 321 in all, with 65 killed, 218 wounded, and 38 missing. [32]

Although the Americans believed they had dealt Burgoyne a significant blow, they realized that his army was still very dangerous and braced themselves for another attack. Fortunately for the Americans -- who were very low on ammunition -- it never materialized.

General Burgoyne actually planned to resume his advance on September 20th, but canceled at the last minute to rest his troops. While they rested, Burgoyne received news that General Henry Clinton was leading a British detachment northward from New York to attack the American posts in the New York Highlands and draw some of the Americans way

---

[29] Anburey, 175
[30] Wilkinson, Appendix D
[31] Ibid.
[32] Ibid.

from Bemis Heights. Although Clinton's force was too small to fight its way to General Burgoyne, both generals hoped that Clinton's presence would force General Gates to send some of this troops south and give Burgoyne a better chance to break through to Albany.

General Burgoyne decided to fortify his position and wait for Clinton's advance to have the desired effect. Unfortunately for Burgoyne, few Americans left Bemis Heights. In fact, during the seventeen day standoff, the American army swelled to over 10,000 men.[33]

With time on his side, the ever cautious Gates waited behind his fortified lines. Every passing day saw Burgoyne's supplies dwindle, and his situation grow more desperate. Colonel Morgan's light corps added to Burgoyne's discomfort by constantly harassing his lines and foraging parties. General Burgoyne acknowledged Morgan's impact in a letter:

> From the 20th of September to the 7th of October, the armies were so near, that not a single night passed without firing, and sometimes concerted attacks upon our advanced picquets; no foraging party could be made without great detachments to cover it; it was the plan of the enemy to harass the army by constant alarms, and their superiority of numbers enabled them to attempt it without fatigue to themselves. [34]

The value of Morgan's riflemen was highlighted in an exchange of letters between General Washington and General Gates. On September 24th, General Washington congratulated Gates on his success at Freeman's Farm. He then requested the return of Morgan's riflemen to the main army:

---

[33] Wilkinson, "A General Return of the Army of the United States, commanded by the Hon. Major-General Horatio Gates, 4 Oct. 1777," Appendix E

[34] Burgoyne, 168

This Army has not been able to oppose General Howe's with the success that was wished, and needs a Reinforcement. I therefore request, if you have been so fortunate, as to Oblige General Burgoyne to retreat to Tyconderoga—or If you have not and circumstances will admit, that you will Order Colo. Morgan to Join me again with his Corps. I sent him up when I thought you materially wanted him, and if his services can be dispensed with now, you will direct his return immediately. [35]

The fact that Washington requested only the Rifle Corps's return is a testament of his high regard for the unit. General Gates's response was equally telling of his esteem and reliance on the riflemen:

Since the Action of the 19th Instant, the Enemy have kept the Ground they Occupied the Morning of that Day, And fortified their Camp. The Advanced Centrys of my picquets, are posted within Shot, And Opposite the Enemy's; neither side have given Ground an Inch. In this Situation, Your Excellency would not wish me to part with the Corps the Army of General Burgoyne are most Afraid of. [36]

General Gates added that, with British provisions dwindling, it was only a matter of days or weeks before Burgoyne either risked another battle or withdrew to Ticonderoga. Gates was confident of success, and informed Washington that he hoped to soon send far more than one regiment as reinforcements. [37]

---

[35] "General Washington to General Gates, 24 September, 1777," *The Papers of George Washington, Vol. 11*, 310
[36] "General Gates to General Washington, 5 October, 1777," *The Papers of George Washington, Vol. 11*, 392
[37] Ibid.

The day after he wrote to Washington, General Gates ordered the light corps, along with 400 additional troops, to reconnoiter the enemy's lines. They circled around to the rear of the British and captured seven prisoners.[38] Major Dearborn reported,

> *As we Returned, Night comeing on, together with a heavy Rain, we got Bewildered in the woods & Stayed all night.*[39]

While Morgan's light corps endured a miserable night in the field, the critical British supply situation finally forced General Burgoyne to act. He decided to probe the American position with a large reconnaissance detachment. If the reconnaissance discovered a weakness in the American lines, he would follow with an attack the next day. If no weakness was found, the army would retreat to Fort Ticonderoga.

Battle of Bemis Heights

General Burgoyne's reconnaissance force numbered approximately 1,500 men and ten cannon.[40] Although nearly all of the army's units contributed men, the bulk came from the right wing of Burgoyne's line. Two redoubts anchored this position. One was manned by British light infantry under Lieutenant Colonel Balcarress. The other was defended by German grenadiers under Lieutenant Colonel Breymann. Since the march route of the reconnaissance detachment placed it between the Americans and the redoubts, General

---

[38] Dearborn Journal, 108

[39] Ibid.

[40] Eric Schnitzer, "Battling for the Saratoga Landscape," *Cultural Landscape Report: Saratoga Battle, Saratoga National Park, Vol. 1* (Boston, MA: Olmsted Center for Landscape Preservation), 44

Burgoyne drew heavily from these fortifications and left only a skeleton force in each.[41]

Burgoyne led his troops out of camp around noon and slowly advanced toward the American left wing. His skirmishers drove off American picquets less than a mile into their march. Burgoyne halted at the Barber farm and posted his men in a long line facing the Americans. The British right flank, composed of light infantry troops, rested in a clearing at the base of a wooded hill. German troops, supported by artillery, held the center of the line, and the left was defended by British grenadiers and artillery.[42]

General Burgoyne tried to observe the American line from Barber's farm, but the woods obscured his view. Ironically, as Burgoyne and his staff struggled to peer through the woods, they were observed by an American officer.

When reports of Burgoyne's advance reached American headquarters, General Gates dispatched his aide, Lieutenant Colonel Wilkinson, to investigate:

> I perceived about half a mile from the line of our encampment, several columns of the enemy, 60 or 70 rods from me, entering a wheat field which had not been cut, and was separated from me by a small rivulet...After entering the field, they displayed, formed the line, and sat down in double ranks with their arms between their legs. Foragers then proceeded to cut the wheat or standing straw, and I soon after observed several officers, mounted on the top of a cabin, from whence their glasses they were endeavoring to reconnoitre our left, which was concealed from their view by intervening woods.[43]

---

[41] Ibid.
[42] Luzader, 52
[43] Wilkinson, 267

Wilkinson reported his findings to General Gates, who sent Wilkinson to Colonel Morgan with instructions to *"begin the game."* [44] Wilkinson recalled,

> *I waited on the Colonel, whose corps was formed in front of our centre, and delivered the order; he knew the ground, and inquired the position of the enemy: they were formed across a newly cultivated field, their grenadiers with several pieces on the left, bordering on a wood and a small ravine...their light infantry on the right, covered by a worm fence at the foot of the hill...thickly covered with wood; their centre composed of British and German battalions. Colonel Morgan, with his usual sagacity, proposed to make a circuit with his corps by our left, and under cover of the wood to gain the height on the right of the enemy, and from thence commence his attack, so soon as our fire should be opened against their left.* [45]

General Gates approved Morgan's proposal and ordered Poor's brigade to attack Burgoyne's left flank. General Learned's brigade followed with instructions to strike the center of the enemy line.

As Colonel Morgan's men hurried to gain possession of the wooded hill overlooking Burgoyne's right flank, fighting erupted on the left. The intensity of the engagement caused some in Morgan's corps to worry that the Americans were losing. Major Dearborn recalled,

> *Our light troops moved on with a quick step in the course directed, and after ascending the woody hill to a small field about 500 yards to the right of the Enemies main line, we discovered a body of British light Infantry handsomely posted on a ridge 150*

---

[44] Ibid. 268
[45] Ibid.

yards from the edge of the wood where we then were. At this time the fire of the two main armies was unusually heavy and we were apprehensive from the fire that our line was giving way. [46]

Colonel Morgan rushed his men towards the enemy flank. Captain Thomas Posey of Virginia described what happened:

They [the enemy] *had repulsed* [General] *Arnold twice before Morgan made his attack, which was on the right wing of* [the] *enemy – the* [rifle] *regiment had march'd under cover of a thick wood, and a ridge, which ridge the enemy were about to take possession of as Morgan gained the summit of it, the enemy being within good rifle shot, the regiment poured in a well directed fire which brought almost every officer on horseback to the ground.* [47]

Lieutenant Colonel Richard Butler noted the impact of the riflemen in the attack:

I had the Honour to lead the Corps of Riflemen Against their Right wing Under Morgan, Who Commanded in Center of the Whole, our light troops About 1000, & Can say without Ostenation that we saved the day by our timely & vigourous Attack (I believe the Indian Hoop helped A little) as we broke the Right Wing of the Enemy took two 12 Pounders & one six and turned them on them. [48]

---

[46] Dearborn Memoir, 7

[47] Posey Biography

[48] "Lt. Col. Richard Butler to Col. James Wilson, 22 January, 1778," Gratz Collection, Case 4, Box 11, Historical Society of Pennsylvania

Burgoyne's Initial Deployment
On October 7th

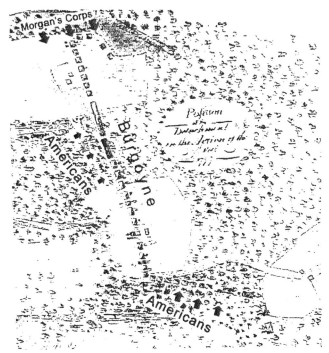

Adapted by Lena Assad

122

Lieutenant Colonel Wilkinson credited Morgan's riflemen and Dearborn's light infantry with routing Burgoyne's right flank:

> *True to his purpose, Morgan at this critical moment poured down like a torrent from the hill, and attacked the right of the enemy in front and flank. Dearborn at the moment, when the enemy's light infantry were attempting to change front,* [to face the riflemen] *pressed forward with ardour and delivered a close fire; then lept the fence, shouted, charged and gallantly forced them in disorder.* [49]

The situation was no better for Burgoyne on his left flank, where his grenadiers were decimated by General Poor's men.

Despite the collapse of his flanks, Burgoyne's center held firm. Furthermore, the commander of the British right flank, General Fraser, worked hard to restore the line. His efforts abruptly ended, however, when one of Morgan's riflemen shot him from his horse. Fraser died the next day.

The pressure on the center of Burgoyne's line soon proved too great, and it joined the rest of the detachment in retreat. Eight British cannon and scores of men were abandoned on the field. Lt. Colonel Wilkinson described the carnage:

> *The ground which had been occupied by the British grenadiers presented a scene of complicated horror and exultation. In the square space of twelve or fifteen yards lay eighteen grenadiers in the agonies of death, and three officers propped up against stumps of trees, two of them mortally wounded, bleeding, and almost speechless.* [50]

---

[49] Wilkinson, 268
[50] Wilkinson, 270

Most of Burgoyne's detachment, including 300 German grenadiers who were drawn from Breymann's redoubt, retreated to the Balcarres redoubt. This bolstered the defenders there, but left Breymann's redoubt (on the extreme right of the British line) undermanned and vulnerable. Two fortified cabins between the redoubts were also weakly manned because of the failure of soldiers to return to them.

Initially these vulnerable positions were not a problem for the British because the Americans concentrated their attack on the Balcarres redoubt. British Corporal Roger Lamb recalled,

> *General Arnold with a brigade of continental troops, pushed rapidly forward, for that part of the camp possessed by lord Balcarres, at the head of the British light infantry, and some of the line; here they were received by a heavy and well directed fire which moved down their ranks, and compelled them to retreat in disorder.* [51]

About three hundred yards to the right, Colonel Morgan's corps prepared to storm the Breymann redoubt.

Morgan's men had advanced very close to the redoubt and used a steep hill in their front to protect them from enemy fire.[52] Lieutenant Colonel Wilkinson described the scene:

> *The Germans were encamped immediately behind the rail breast-work, and the ground in front of it declined in a very gentle slope for about 120 yards, when it sunk abruptly; our troops had formed a line under this declivity, and covered breast high were warmly engaged with the Germans.* [53]

---

[51] Lamb, 164
[52] Schnitzer, 50
[53] Wilkinson, 272

Barcarres & Breymann Redoubts

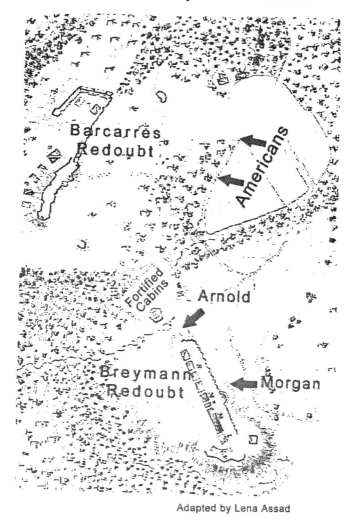

Adapted by Lena Assad

Morgan was reinforced by General Learned's brigade. Wilkinson recommended that General Learned attack a weak spot in the enemy line, the two sparsely manned cabins:

> I had particularly examined the ground between the left of the Germans and the light infantry, occupied by the provincialists, from whence I had observed a slack fire; I therefore recommended to General Learned to incline to his right, and attack at that point: he did so with great gallantry; the provincialists abandoned their position and fled; the German flank was by this means uncovered. [54]

Learned's brigade was joined by General Benedict Arnold, who, without orders, assumed command of the attack. Colonel Wilkinson recalled that Arnold

> Dashed to the left through the fire of the two lines and escaped unhurt; he then turned the right of the enemy, as I was informed by that most excellent officer, Colonel Butler, and collecting 15 or 20 riflemen threw himself with this party into the rear of the enemy, just as they gave way, where his leg was broke, and his horse killed under him. [55]

Lieutenant Colonel Richard Butler's account of the assault was similar:

> Genl. Arnold was the first who Entered, one Major Morris with about 12 of the Rifle men followed him on the Rear of their Right Flank while I led up the rest of the Riflemen in front. I was the 3rd officer in [the redoubt]. [56]

---

[54] Ibid.

[55] Ibid., 272

[56] "Lt. Col. Richard Butler to Col. James Wilson, 22 January, 1778,"

Major Dearborn's light infantry also participated in the assault of the redoubt. He described it in his memoirs:

> *The assault was commenced by the advance of Arnold with about 200 men through a cops of wood which covered the Enemies right, the appearance of Arnold on the right was the signal for us to advance and assault the front. The whole was executed in the most spirited and prompted manner and as soon as the Enemy had given us one fire, he fell back from his work to his line of tents, and as we entered he gave way and retreated in confusion.* [57]

As Morgan's light corps swarmed over the walls and through the sally port and embrasures, General Arnold struck the German rear.

Whether by design or chance, the assault on Breymann's redoubt was masterfully executed, and the Germans were quickly overwhelmed. General Burgoyne's line was breeched, and only nightfall saved the British from further disaster.

Once again, the American army had punished the enemy, inflicting far more casualties than they had suffered. This decisive victory left General Burgoyne with only one choice, retreat. His march to Albany was over. It remained to be seen whether his retreat to Fort Ticonderoga would succeed.

Retreat and Surrender

Under cover of darkness, General Burgoyne withdrew his army across the Great Ravine and established a new position on a hill overlooking the Hudson River. The position was called the Great Redoubt, and its location allowed Burgoyne to consolidate his troops and protect the river transports and hospital.

---

[57] Dearborn Memoir, 8

When the Americans realized that Burgoyne had withdrawn across the ravine, they took possession of his old lines and commenced a steady, but ineffectual, bombardment. General Gates sent Morgan's light corps forward to reconnoiter the enemy's rear and harass them. Major Dearborn participated in this reconnaissance:

This morning [Oct. 8] the Rifle men & Light Infantry & several other Regiments march'd in the Rear of the Enimy Expecting they ware Retreeting But found they ware Not. there has Been scurmishing all Day...a Large Number of the Enimy Deserted to us to Day.[58]

General Burgoyne realized that retreat or surrender were the only options left for his army. The former was tremendously difficult, but the latter was still unthinkable. Thus, on the evening of October 8th, Burgoyne began a retreat northward. Over 400 men, too injured or sick to transport, were left under a flag of truce to the care of the Americans. The rest of Burgoyne's army slowly trudged towards Saratoga.

After a few miles, they halted to rest and wait for the boats to catch up. A heavy rain pelted the men all day, and when they resumed their march, the road turned to mud. They arrived at the heights of Saratoga after dark and collapsed on the ground in exhaustion. Lieutenant Digby described the scene:

We remained all night under constant, heavy rain without fires or any kind of shelter to guard us from the inclemency of the weather. It was impossible to sleep, even had we an inclination to do so from the cold and rain....[59]

---

[58] Dearborn Journal, 109
[59] Digby, 300

Ensign Anburey gave an equally distressing account of the British army's first night in Saratoga:

> *The army...arrived at Saratoga, in such a state of fatigue that the men had not strength or inclination to cut wood and make fires, but rather sought sleep in their wet clothes and on the wet ground.* [60]

Despite Burgoyne's slow retreat, the Americans struggled to keep pace. The rain turned the road into a quagmire of mud, and the size of the American army, over 12,000 strong, complicated logistics. Fortunately for the Americans, Burgoyne's retreat ceased at Saratoga.

Over the next few days, as General Burgoyne grappled with his situation, the American riflemen and light infantry constantly harassed them. A steady artillery bombardment added to their discomfort. By October 14th, General Burgoyne and his army had had enough. With his officer's consent, Burgoyne asked for terms of surrender. General Gates was generous in his demands, and on October 17th, General Burgoyne formally surrendered his army.

The most decisive battle of the Revolutionary War to date was over, and Colonel Morgan's riflemen played a crucial role in the victory.

---

[60] Anburey, 190

Chapter Six

Philadelphia Campaign : 1777-78

While Colonel Morgan and his riflemen celebrated their victory at Saratoga, General Washington's army sat outside of Philadelphia. Washington's troops had struggled for weeks to defend the city, losing two hard fought battles in the process. The Americans fought well, but bad weather, intelligence, and luck undermined their effort.

Washington's troops first confronted the British in early September at Cooches Bridge, Delaware. General Howe had landed his army at Head of Elk, Maryland in late August in an effort to outmaneuver Washington. As the British slowly made their way north towards Philadelphia, Washington posted most of his army along a creek and sent an improvised light infantry corps forward to observe. The light troops were commanded by General William Maxwell and consisted of one hundred picked men from each brigade (approximately 700 in total). A number of riflemen, including Captain Charles Porterfield and Lieutenant John Marshall of the 11th Virginia, served in the light corps. Lieutenant Colonel Armand's independent corps, which included riflemen under Captain Antoine Selin, also joined Maxwell's detachment. They were recalled to Wilmington, Delaware on September 2nd, however, when local residents complained to General Washington about their conduct.[1]

Washington's instructions to General Maxwell were clear:

---

[1] "General Washington to General Maxwell, 2 September, 1777," *The Papers of George Washington, Vol. 11,*

*I wish you very much to have the situation of the
Enemy critically reconnoitered, to know as exactly as
possible how and where they lie, in what places they
are approachable; where their several guards are
stationed, and the strength of them; and everything
necessary to be known to enable us to judge, with
precision, whether any advantage may be taken of
their present divided state. No pains should be
omitted to gain as much certainty, as can be had, in
all these particulars.*[2]

The Battle of Cooches Bridge

General Washington expected the British to advance via
Cooches Bridge. He told General Maxwell that his men
*"should...lie quiet and still, and ought to be posted early
tonight, as the Enemy will most probably move...between two
and three O'clock."*[3] After three uneventful days, the British
approached Maxwell's position.

The route to the bridge was ideally situated for the type of
fighting General Maxwell desired. Aware that his detachment
was greatly outnumbered, Maxwell planned to harass and
delay their march with a series of ambushes. His men were
instructed to strike the enemy from concealed positions and
when pressed, fall back, reform, and hit them again. Every
tree, thicket, and rock along the road was a possible firing
position for the Americans. British Captain John Montresor
ominously described the terrain in his journal:

---

[2] "General Washington to General William Maxwell, 3 September, 1777,"
The Papers of George Washington, Vol. 11, 140
[3] Ibid. 95

> *The Country is close-- the woods within shot of the road, frequently in front and flank and in projecting points towards the Road.*[4]

Captain Johann Ewald, with six dragoons, rode ahead of the British advance corps. As they cautiously approached Maxwell's position shots rang out from the nearby wood. Ewald recalled,

> *I...had not gone a hundred paces from the advance guard when I received fire from a hedge, through which these six men* [the dragoons] *were all either killed or wounded. My horse, which normally was well used to fire, reared so high several times that I expected it would throw me. I cried out, "Foot jagers forward!" and advanced with them to the area from which the fire was coming...At this moment I ran into another enemy party with which I became heavily engaged. Lieutenant Colonel von Wurmb, who came with the entire Corps assisted by the light infantry, ordered the advance guard to be supported.*[5]

The Americans, according to plan, fell back. *"A Continued Smart irregular fire* [ensued] *for near two miles,"* reported Captain Montresor.[6]

The engagement lasted into the afternoon with the Americans fighting from tree to tree. They gradually withdrew to Iron Hill and Cooches Bridge. General Howe ordered the British advance guard to drive the enemy off the hill. Captain Ewald led the way:

---

[4] "Journal of Captain John Montresor, 3 September, 1777," *The Pennsylvania Magazine of History and Biography Vol. 5,* (Philadelphia: The Historical Society of Pennsylvania, 1881), 412
[5] Ewald, 77
[6] Montressor Journal, 412

The charge was sounded, and the enemy was attacked so severely and with such spirit by the jagers that we became masters of the mountain after a seven hour engagement.[7]

Ewald described the fight as intense:

The majority of the jagers came to close quarters with the enemy, and the hunting sword was used as much as the rifle... The jagers alone enjoyed the honor of driving the enemy out of his advantageous position.[8]

Although the Americans were forced from Iron Hill, they still held the bridge. Sergeant Thomas Sullivan, of the British 49th Regiment, observed,

After a hot fire the enemy retreated towards their main body, by Iron Hill. They made a stand at the Bridge for some time, but the pursuing Corps made them quit that post also, and retire with loss.[9]

By mid-afternoon General Maxwell withdrew from Cooches Bridge and rejoined the main army. Despite their retreat, Maxwell's Corps performed their mission admirably. They delayed Howe's advance and harassed his troops to the point that although there were still many hours of daylight left, Howe opted to halt his march and rest his troops.[10]

---

[7] Ewald, 77

[8] Ibid.

[9] "Before and After the Battle of Brandywine: Extracts from the Journal of Sergeant Thomas Sullivan of H.M. Forty-Ninth Regiment of Foot," 3 September, 1777 in *The Pennsylvania Magazine of History and Biography, Vol. 31*, (Philadelphia: Historical Society of Pennsylvania, 410

[10] Montressor Journal, 413

General Washington was pleased with the conduct of the light corps and reported to Congress that Maxwell's detachment inflicted considerable damage on the enemy. He particularly noted the role of Maxwell's riflemen:

This morning the Enemy came out with considerable force and three pieces of Artillery, against our Light advanced Corps, and after some pretty smart skirmishing obliged them to retreat, being far inferior in number and without Cannon. The loss on either side is not yet ascertained. Our's, tho not exactly known, is not very considerable; Theirs, we have reason to believe, was much greater, as some of our parties composed of expert Marksmen, had Opportunities of giving them several, close, well directed Fires, more particularly in One instant, when a body of Riflemen formed a kind of Ambuscade.[11]

Accurate casualty figures for Cooches Bridge are difficult to determine. Both sides claimed they inflicted more loss on the enemy than they sustained. It appears, however, that the losses were rather low, ranging between twenty-five to fifty men each.[12]

---

[11] "General Washington to John Hancock, 3 September 1777," *The Papers of George Washington, Vol. 11*, 135

[12] General Howe reported losses of 3 dead and 21 wounded. Sergeant Thomas Sullivan reported identical numbers in his journal. Captain Ewald, however, claimed losses of 11 dead and 45 wounded. The reports of American losses also vary. Captain Montresor claimed that, "*the rebels left about 20 dead*". Major Baurmeister put that number at 30. Captain Muenchhausen claimed 41 rebels were buried by the British, including five officers. For his part, General Washington reported to Congress that, "*...we had forty killed and wounded, and as our own Men were thinly posted they must have done more damage upon a close Body then they received.*"

Maxwell's Corps joined the American army at Red Clay Creek. They took up a new position in advance of the army and were ordered to maintain a close watch on the enemy.[13] Two days after the skirmish, General Washington gave General Maxwell the following instructions:

> *I should be glad to hear how the Enemy are situated and what they seem to be about. Send out reconnoitering parties under good intelligent officers to inspect the different parts of their Camp, and gain as exact an insight as possible into their circumstances...You should always have small advanced parties towards the Enemy's lines, about the hour of the morning you expect them to move, as it is of essential importance to us, to have the earliest intelligence of it.*[14]

There was little to report, however, as the British remained inactive for the next three days.

The situation changed on September 7th. Reports reached General Washington that the British were about to march. Washington ordered his army to prepare to do likewise:

> *The General has received a confirmation...that the enemy have disencumbered themselves of all their baggage, even to their tents, reserving only their blankets and such part of the cloathing as is absolutely necessary. This indicates a speedy & rapid movement, and points out the necessity of following the example, and ridding ourselves for a few days of every thing we can possibly dispense with...Officers should only retain their blankets,*

---

[13] Reed, 89

[14] "General Washington to General William Maxwell, 5 September, 1777," *The Papers of George Washington Vol. 11,* 154

great coats, and three or four shirts of under cloaths, and the men should, besides what they have on, keep only a Blanket, and a shirt a piece, and such as have it, a great coat – All trunks, chests, boxes, other bedding, and cloathes... [are] to be sent away, 'till the elapsing of a few days shall determine whether the enemy mean an immediate attack, or not.[15]

Another day passed before General Howe's intentions became clear. Rather than confront the Americans in a costly frontal assault of their entrenched position, General Howe marched north in an attempt to gain the right flank of the Americans.

Determined to protect both his flank and Philadelphia, General Washington raced his army northward. His destination was Chadd's Ford, the likely British crossing point over Brandywine Creek. The Americans marched with urgency and arrived at the ford on September 9th.

Advance elements of General Howe's army arrived at Kennett Square, seven miles west of Chadd's Ford, that same evening. General Howe, with the main portion of his army, arrived the next morning. He rested his men on September 10th, and devised an attack plan for the next day. The stage was set for a major clash, and the fate of Philadelphia hung in the balance.

---

[15] "General Orders for 7 September, 1777," *The Papers of George Washington, Vol. 11*, 167-168

Brandywine

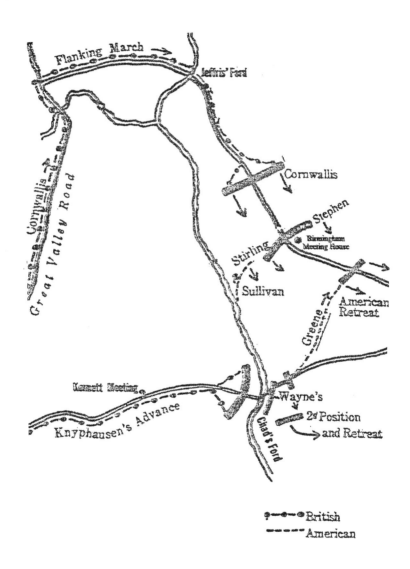

Adapted by Lena Assad

Battle of Brandywine

With only a few miles separating the two armies, General Washington once again turned to Maxwell's light infantry corps to act as his eyes and ears. Augmented by the addition of local militia, the corps numbered around 800 men.[16] It was sent across the Brandywine to screen the army and reconnoiter the approaches to Chadd's Ford.[17] General Maxwell positioned a large portion of his men, as well as a few light cannon, on a ridge overlooking the west bank of the Brandywine and the road leading to the ford.[18] He placed smaller detachments closer to the enemy. Horse patrols extended almost to Kennett Square with orders to sound the alarm when the enemy approached.

The British commenced their march towards the Americans at daybreak on September 11th, 1777.[19] They marched in two separate columns along two separate roads.[20] General Howe, with over 8,000 men, headed north on a seventeen mile trek to gain the right flank of the American army.[21] General Knyphausen, with just under 7,000 men, marched east, straight towards the American army at Chadd's Ford.[22] His column was a decoy, or holding force. General Howe hoped to duplicate his success at Long Island by feigning a frontal attack and striking the Americans on their vulnerable flank. Timing and deception were key elements of the plan. General

---

[16] Samuel Smith, *The Battle of Brandywine,* (Monmouth Beach, NJ: Philip Freneau Press, 1976), 9

[17] Reed, 113

[18] Samuel Smith, *The Battle of Brandywine,* 10

[19] Sullivan Journal, 412

[20] Bernard Uhlendorf and Edna Vosper, eds., "Letters of Major Baurmeister During the Philadelphia Campaign," *The Pennsylvania Magazine of History and Biography, Vol. 59,* (Philadelphia: Historical Society of Pennsylvania, 1935), 404

[21] Smith, 9

[22] Ibid.

Knyphausen had to convince the Americans that his force was the main assault.

Knyphausen's vanguard encountered a few American horsemen less than a mile into their march and easily dispersed them with no loss to either side.[23]   The first deadly encounter occurred soon afterwards.   As the British approached Kennett Meetinghouse, they were attacked by Captain Charles Porterfield's detachment.   Lieutenant Colonel William Heth of the 11th Virginia described Porterfield's role in the engagement:

> *Our valuable Friend Porterfield began the action*
> *with day light – he killed (himself) the first man who*
> *fell that day – His conduct through the whole day –*
> *was such, as has acquired him the greatest Honor –*
> *A great proportion of British Officers fell by a party*
> *under his command & Capt. Waggoners (who is a*
> *brave officer) and I find it impossible to conceal my*
> *pride, from having in possession an Elegant double*
> *gilted mounted small sword -- a Trophy of their*
> *success.*[24]

Despite the initial shock of the ambush, the British rapidly advanced and forced Captain Porterfield to withdraw to the next American position.   Knyphausen's advance corps pressed forward, but met steady resistance all the way.   Sergeant Thomas Sullivan of Britain's 49th Regiment noted that,

---

[23] Bruce E. Moway, *September 11, 1777: Washington's Defeat at Brandywine Dooms Philadelphia*, (PA: White Mane Books, 2002), 84

[24] B. Floyd Flickinger, "Heth to Morgan, 2 October 1777," in "The Diary of Lieutenant William Heth while a Prisoner in Quebec, 1776", *Annual Papers of the Winchester Historical Society*, (Winchester: The Society, 1931), 33

The enemys Light infantry and Riflemen kept up a running fire, mixed with regular vollies, for 5 miles.[25]

As Knyphausen's advance guard neared Brandywine Creek, they descended a long hill and approached a portion of the road that passed through marshy land. Woods and hills bordered the road, providing plenty of cover for Maxwell's troops.[26] *"Heretofore the enemy had been repulsed by our vanguard alone,"* wrote Baurmeister, *"but now the engagement became more serious..."*[27]

The fire from Maxwell's infantry and cannon forced General Knyphausen to send a brigade forward to reinforce his depleted advance corps. Artillery was also placed on a nearby hill and commenced firing on the Americans in the woods and behind their hastily built breastworks. Sergeant Thomas Sullivan recalled,

We played upon them with two 6 pounders for half an hour and drove them out of the breastworks, which was made of loose wood upon the declivity of the hill.[28]

Major Baurmeister gave a more detailed account of this part of the battle:

The Queen's Rangers...proceeded to the left and after a short but very rapid musketry-fire, supported by the 23rd English Regiment...drove the rebels out of their woods and straight across the lowland. Under cover of a continuous cannonade, the 28th English

---

[25] Henry Lee, *The Revolutionary War Memoirs of General Henry Lee* New York: Da Capo Press, 1998, (Originally published in 1812 as, *Memoirs of the War in the Southern Department of the United States*), 89
[26] Ibid.
[27] Ibid.
[28] Sullivan Journal, 413

Regiment went off to the right of the column, and soon the rebels, who had been shouting "Hurrah" and firing briskly from a gorge in front of us, were quickly put to flight.[29]

Sergeant Sullivan, positioned near the center of the attack, recounted the final push that forced Maxwell's light corps across the Brandywine:

As we crossed the brook [Ring Run] they formed behind another fence at a field's distance, from whence we soon drove 'em, and a Battalion of Hessians, which formed at the left of our Brigade, fell in with them as they retreated...and after a smart pursuit...they [the Americans] crossed the Brandywine and took up post on that side; leaving a few men killed and a few more wounded behind.[30]

It was about 10:30 in the morning when the last of Maxwell's men crossed the Brandywine and rejoined the American army.[31] They were tired after three hours of intense fighting. Yet, their losses were surprisingly light.[32]

For the next six hours, each side remained relatively still. Knyphausen's detachment waited for General Howe's signal to attack, and the Americans waited for Knyphausen to force a passage across the Brandywine. Lieutenant John Marshall, who was attached to Maxwell's Corps, noted that, during the lull, small parties of Americans crossed the creek. Scattered firing occurred all day but to little effect.[46] One such incident, however, involving a party of men (probably riflemen) under

---

[29] Baurmeister Letters, 405
[30] Sullivan Journal, 413-414
[31] Baurmeister Letters, 406
[32] Flickinger, "William Heth to Col. Daniel Morgan, 30 September, 1777," in "The Diary of Lieutenant William Heth while a Prisoner in Quebec, 1777," 31
[46] Ibid.

Captains Porterfield and Waggoner, proved costly to the British. According to Marshall, Captains Porterfield and Waggoner led a detachment across the creek that,

> *Engaged the British flank guard very closely, killed a captain with ten or fifteen privates, drove them from the wood, and were on the point of taking a field piece. The sharpness of the skirmish soon drew a large body of the British to that quarter, and the Americans were again driven over the Brandywine.*[33]

Sergeant Thomas Sullivan may have described the same encounter in his diary:

> *A company of the 28th and a company of our Regiment advanced upon the hill to the right of the Ford, and in front of the enemy's left flank, in order to divert them, who were posted at a hundred yards distance in their front, behind trees, to the amount of 500, all chosen marksmen. A smart fire maintained on both sides for two hours, without either parties quitting their posts. Out of the two companies there were about 20 men killed and wounded...and two 6 pounders were ordered up the hill to dislodge the enemy if possible...These guns played upon them for some time, but they were so concealed under cover of the trees, that it was to no purpose...The guns were ordered back and also the two companies in order to draw the enemy after them from the trees, which scheme had the desired effect, for they quitted their post and advanced to the top of the hill where they were attacked [by] four companies of the 10th Battalion, in front, while the 40th made a charge upon*

---

[33] Ibid. 300

their left flank, by going round the hill, and put them
to an immediate rout.[34]

It is difficult to determine whether the two accounts are of the same incident. Nonetheless, it is clear that skirmishing continued near Chadd's Ford all day, and American riflemen were heavily involved.

At American headquarters, conflicting reports of British troop movements concerned General Washington. Initial reports suggested that General Howe had divided his army and was vulnerable to attack. Washington saw an opportunity and ordered Generals Sullivan and Greene to cross the creek and attack. Before they commenced the assault, however, new reports prompted Washington to question the accuracy of the earlier intelligence. If the initial reports were wrong, and Howe had not divided his army, then Sullivan and Greene risked confronting a vastly superior foe. The situation was too uncertain, so Washington cancelled the attack.

By early afternoon, however, it was clear that the British were indeed moving against the American right. Since it was too late to take the offensive, Washington ordered Generals Sullivan, Stirling, and Stephen, to change their division fronts along Brandywine Creek and re-deploy a few miles away, near the Birmingham Meeting House. General Stirling and Stephen arrived ahead of Sullivan's division and immediately deployed on the hills to the southwest of the Meeting House. A mile to the north, thousands of British and German troops prepared to attack.

Holding the right flank of the new American position was Brigadier General William Woodford's brigade of Virginians. It was placed on a hill about three hundred yards southwest of the Birmingham Meeting House. Woodford's position meant that his own right flank was uncovered. To protect it he sent his most experienced regiment, the 170 men of the 3rd

---

[34] Sullivan Journal, 414

Virginia, to occupy an orchard a hundred yards north of the Meeting House. This placed them nearly 400 yards away from the American line.

Prior to General Howe's attack, the rest of Woodford's brigade was redeployed to the right and rear. General George Weedon of Virginia recalled,

> *In making this Alteration, unfavorable Ground, made it necessary for Woodford to move his Brigade 200 Paces back of the Line & threw Marshall's wood in his front.*[35]

The 3rd Virginia was now over 500 yards in front of the main American line and very isolated. Yet the men held firm and awaited the attack.

The battle began around 3:30 p.m. when the British advance guard, comprised of German jaegers, British dragoons, and light infantry, advanced towards the orchard. As they neared it, they *"received the fire from about 200 men in an orchard."*[36] This unexpected resistance caused them to take cover behind a fence, two hundred paces from the 3rd Virginia.[37] Captain Johann Ewald, commanding the British advance force, described the encounter:

> *About half past three I caught sight of some infantry and horsemen behind a village on a hill in the distance. I drew up at once and deployed...I reached the first houses of the village with the flankers of the jagers, and Lt. Hagen followed me with the horsemen. But unfortunately for us, the time this took favored the enemy and I received extremely heavy small-arms fire from the gardens and houses,*

---

[35] Ibid.
[36] Smith, 16
[37] Ibid. 17

*through which, however, only two jaegers were
sounded. Everyone ran back, and I formed them
again behind the fences or walls at a distance of two
hundred paces from the village...* [38]

American artillery and small arms fire was so intense at the
orchard that the main British battle line also briefly halted
there. One British officer reported,

*The trees [were] cracking over ones head. The
branches riven by the artillery, the leaves falling as
in autumn by the grapeshot.* [39]

The British resumed the attack and pushed the Virginians
out of the orchard. Colonel Thomas Marshall re-positioned his
men about one hundred paces to the rear, behind a stone wall
at the Birmingham Meeting House. Sheltered by the wall, the
3rd Virginia maintained a heavy fire on the British. Marshall's
men could not hold their position indefinitely, however. [40]
With more than a quarter of his troops out of action and the
enemy pressing his front and both flanks, Colonel Marshall
had no choice but to retreat.

At Chadd's Ford, Maxwell's light corps heard the fight on
the right flank -- so did General Knyphausen and his men. It
was the signal for Knyphausen to resume his attack. Chadd's
Ford was defended by General Anthony Wayne's division,
General William Maxwell's light corps, and Colonel Thomas
Proctor's battery of artillery. General Nathanael Greene's
division of Virginians, consisting of General Weedon's and
General Muhlenberg's brigades, was originally stationed
nearby as a reserve. When fighting erupted at Birmingham,
General Washington ordered Greene to rush his men there.

---

[38] Ewald Journal, 84-85
[39] Smith, 17
[40] Ibid.

Greene's departure left the Americans at Chadd's Ford outnumbered.

Around 5:00 p.m., General Knyphausen commenced a *"fearful cannonade"* to soften up the Americans.[41] Fifteen minutes later, he halted the bombardment and sent his infantry across the creek.[42] Captain Ewald recalled that Knyphausen's force,

> *Waded through the creek...which is about fifty paces wide and a half-man deep, under grapeshot and small-arms fire.*[43]

When they reached the other side, Knyphausen's men pressed forward. Sergeant Sullivan described the action:

> *The enemy's cannon...*[misfired] *as they crossed, and before the gunners could fire them off, the men of that Battalion put them to the bayonet, and forced the enemy from the entrenchment, who drawing up in the field and orchard just by, rallied afresh and fought bayonet to bayonet, but the rest of the two Brigades, 71st and Rangers coming up,* [obliged the Americans] *to retreat in the greatest confusion, leaving their artillery and ammunition in the field.*[44]

Maxwell's light corps was positioned a bit to the rear of Chadd's Ford on a hill overlooking the Chester Road.[45] This placed them away from the initial fighting. Knyphausen's force soon advanced down the road and engaged Maxwell's Corps in heavy fighting.[46]

---

[41] Baurmeister Letter, 406
[42] Mowday, 143
[43] Ewald Journal, 82
[44] Sullivan Journal, 416-417
[45] Smith, 23
[46] Ibid.

While the Americans struggled with Knyphausen's detachment, the right wing of General Howe's flank attack (at Birmingham) suddenly appeared on Maxwell's right and rear. They had swung too far west and completely missed the fight at Birmingham Heights. Their arrival triggered a disorderly American retreat.[47] Major Baurmeister recalled,

> *Our regiments gained one height after another as the enemy withdrew. They withstood one more rather severe attack behind some houses and ditches in front of their left wing. Finally, we saw the entire enemy line and four guns, which fired frequently, drawn up on another height in front of a dense forest, their right wing resting on the Chester road. By the time it grew dark, the van of the left column of General Howe had joined us...The enemy, however, gained the road to Chester in considerable confusion. Had not darkness favored their retreat, we might have come into possession of much artillery, munitions, and horses.[48]*

The situation for the Americans at Birmingham was no better. The British pushed them off the heights and towards the village of Dillworth. General Greene's division rushed to their aid and arrived in time to cover their retreat.[49] Lieutenant James McMichael, of General Weedon's brigade, described what happened:

> *We took the front and attacked the enemy at 5:30 p.m., and being engaged with their grand army, we at first were obliged to retreat a few yards and formed*

[47] Mowday, 147

[48] Baurmeister Letters, 407

[49] Harry M. Ward, *Duty, Honor, Or Country: General George Weedon and The American Revolution,* (Philadelphia : The American Philosophical Society, 1979), 101

in an open field when we fought without giving way on either side until dark. Our ammunition almost expended, firing ceased on both sides, when we received orders to proceed to Chester...This day for a severe and successive engagement exceeded all I ever saw. Our regiment fought at one stand about an hour under incessant fire, and yet the loss was less than at Long Island; neither were we so near each other as at Princeton, our common distance being about 50 yards.[50]

General Greene's stand near Dillworth allowed the American right wing to withdraw in relative order. They abandoned hundreds of their comrades, eleven cannon, and the battlefield. General Howe suffered only half of the one thousand casualties inflicted on the Americans, and his objective, Philadelphia, lay just a few miles away, defended by a weakened and presumably dispirited enemy. [51]

Yet, the American army was not as weak as Howe assumed. While the Americans were unable to prevent the fall of Philadelphia, they remained a threat to the British. In late September General Washington sought to enhance this threat by restructuring the army. Maxwell's light corps was disbanded, and the men sent back to their units. It is unclear what prompted this. Perhaps accusations of misconduct and lack of initiative from some of Maxwell's subordinates were a factor. Lieutenant Colonel William Heth attacked Maxwell in

---

[50] "Diary of Lieutenant McMichael, 150
[51] Smith, 23

Determining an exact figure of American losses is difficult. Many of those listed as captured, were also listed as wounded, so there was a lot of double counting. The British claimed they buried almost 400 Americans. John Marshall put the number at 300 killed and 600 wounded, of which 300-400 were also captured. This number corresponds with Sergeant Sullivan's report of 300 killed, 600 wounded and 400 captured.

a letter to Colonel Daniel Morgan prior to the corps dissolution:

> *You have been greatly wished for since the Enemies Landing at the Head of Elk – Maxwell's Corps Twas expected would do great things – we had opportunities – and anybody but an old woman would have availd themselves of them – He is to be sure – A Damnd bitch of a General.*[52]

Unlike General Maxwell, Washington could not be accused of being a timid commander. On the morning of October 3rd, he launched a surprise assault against General Howe's troops in the village of Germantown. The complicated attack was initially a success, but it soon unraveled and ended in another American defeat. Washington, discouraged by the setback, withdrew to Whitemarsh, about thirteen miles north of Philadelphia, to regroup. Reinforcements, including Morgan's rifle corps, arrived in mid November.

Morgan's Corps Returns

Morgan's rifle corps began its long march to Whitemarsh just days after Burgoyne's surrender at Saratoga. General Washington was so eager for their return that he sent his aide, Lieutenant Colonel Alexander Hamilton, to New York to expedite their march. Washington told Hamilton that,

> *I expect you will meet Colo: Morgan's Corps on their way down, if you do, let them know how essential their services are to us, and desire the Colo...to hasten their March as much as is consistent with the health of the men....*[53]

---

[52] Heth Diary, 2 October, 1777, 33
[53] "General Washington to Alexander Hamilton, 30 October, 1777," *The Papers of George Washington, Vol. 12,* 61

The rifle corps arrived at Whitemarsh in mid November.[54] The unit's effectiveness was greatly diminished by the hardship of the Saratoga campaign and long march to Pennsylvania. *"There are not more than one hundred and Seventy of Morgan's Corps fit to march, as they in general want Shoes,"* noted General Washington upon their return.[55]

After a brief rest at Whitemarsh, Morgan's corps joined a large American detachment in New Jersey under General Greene. This detachment was originally intended to assist the garrison at Fort Mercer (on the Jersey side of the Delaware River), but the fort was evacuated prior to its arrival. Despite the loss of Fort Mercer, General Greene remained in New Jersey and skirmished with British foraging parties. In late November, the Marquis de La Fayette, a French volunteer in the American army, was involved in one of these skirmishes. Morgan's riflemen, commanded by Lieutenant Colonel Richard Butler, comprised half of La Fayette's force and greatly impressed him. *"The Marquis is charmed with the spirited behaviour of the Militia & Rifle Corps,"* noted General Greene after the skirmish.[56] La Fayette lavished praise on the riflemen in his report to General Washington:

---

[54] "General Washington to General Greene, 22 November, 1777," *The Papers of George Washington, Vol. 12,* 349-350
[55] Ibid.
[56] "General Greene to General Washington, 26 November, 1777," *The Papers of George Washington, Vol. 12,* 409

Pennsylvania

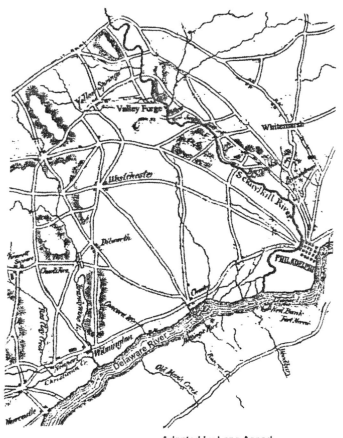

Adapted by Lena Assad

I take the greatest pleasure to let you know that the conduct of our soldiers is above all praises – I never saw men so merry, so spirited, so desirous to go on to the enemy what ever forces they could have as the little party was in this little fight. I found the riflemen above even their reputation...I must tell too the riflemen had been the whole day running before my horse without eating or taking any rest. [57]

On November 28th, General Greene marched the bulk of his force back to Whitemarsh. He left Morgan's corps and a detachment of Virginian cavalry under Captain Henry Lee in New Jersey to bolster the local militia and harass the enemy.[58] They spent another week skirmishing with the British and returned to Whitemarsh in early December, just in time to help fend off General Howe's last major operation of the year.

On the night of December 4th, 10,000 British troops marched towards the American camp at Whitemarsh.[59] The American army, about 12,000 strong, was alerted and manned their fortifications in anticipation of an attack.[60] The British halted at Chestnut Hill, about three miles from Whitemarsh, to assess Washington's deployment. General Washington sent 600 Pennsylvania militia forward to skirmish with Howe's advance parties and obstruct Howe's reconnaissance, but they were easily dispersed.[61]

General Howe decided that the American defenses on the right were too strong to attack, so he shifted his army three

---

[57] "General LaFayette to General Washington, 26 November, 1777," *The Papers of George Washington, Vol. 12*, 418-419
[58] "General Greene to General Washington, 28 November, 1777," *The Papers of George Washington, Vol. 12*, 428
[59] David Martin, *The Philadelphia Campaign, June 1777 – July 1778*, (Da Capa Press, 1993), 160
[60] Lesser, "A General Return of the Continental Army...Dec. 3, 1777," 53
[61] Martin, 161

miles east to probe the American left wing.[62] As they approached the American lines, Washington sent Morgan's rifle corps and the Maryland Militia forward to attack Howe's right flank. The engagement was fierce and cost both sides dearly. Captain Johann Ewald, of the German Jagers, recalled,

> *The light infantry fell into an ambuscade which the American Colonel Morgan and his corps of riflemen had laid in a marshy wood, through which over fifty men and three officers were killed.*[63]

Twenty-seven riflemen also fell that day, including Major Joseph Morris.[64] This distinguished officer was mortally wounded, and his loss was severely felt by the rifle corps.

The Americans expected Howe to launch a full attack the next morning, but the day passed peacefully. The calm continued into the next morning. The British finally moved in the afternoon, but their direction was rearward, towards Philadelphia. General Howe refused to risk his army in an assault on such a strong position. His withdrawal marked an end of the campaign season. The British looked forward to a relatively comfortable winter in Philadelphia. The Americans were not as fortunate.

---

[62] "General Washington to Patrick Henry, 10 December, 1777," *The Papers of George Washington, Vol. 12*, 590
[63] Ewald, 109
[64] "General Washington to Henry Laurens, 10 December, 1777," *The Papers of George Washington, Vol. 12*, 592

Valley Forge

On December 19th, General Washington moved his army into winter quarters at Valley Forge. He wanted to keep the army intact and close enough to Philadelphia to challenge enemy incursions into the countryside. Valley Forge was also an excellent defensive position. The Schuylkill River protected the left flank of the Americans and a steep hill, called Mount Joy, covered their rear. Although the front and right flank of the encampment possessed few natural barriers, the open terrain made an attack from those directions very hazardous.

The soldiers constructed log huts as soon as they arrived. They also built two lines of earthworks and redoubts. The outer line extended along a ridge from the Schuylkill River to the foot of Mount Joy. Most of the army was stationed along this line in rows of huts behind the fortifications. An inner defense line was built along Mount Joy. It also ran to the river.

Washington's troops lacked both clothing and provisions at Valley Forge. On December 22nd, General James Varnum of Rhode Island reported to General Washington:

Three Days successively, we have been destitute of Bread. Two Days we have been intirely without Meat. —It is not to be had from Commissaries. — Whenever we procure Beef, it is of such a vile Quality, as to render it a poor Succedanium for Food. The Men must be supplied, or they cannot be commanded. [65]

General Washington forwarded the bad news to Congress:

---

[65] Joseph Lee Boyle, "General Varnum to General Washington, 22 December, 1777," *Writings from the Valley Forge Encampment of the Continental Army, Vol. 1,* (Bowie: Heritage Books Inc., 2000), 2

I do not know from what cause this alarming deficiency, or rather total failure of Supplies arises: But unless more vigorous exertions and better regulations take place in that line and immediately, This Army must dissolve.[66]

While the main army struggled with supply problems, Morgan's riflemen guarded the approaches to camp. They were posted a few miles south of Valley Forge near the village of Radnor. The riflemen were joined by detachments of cavalry and skirmished with the enemy all winter.[67]

Colonel Morgan returned to Virginia on furlough in January. With Lieutenant Colonel Richard Butler also absent and Major Morris dead, command of the rifle corps fell to Captain Thomas Posey. Posey recalled in his biography that he,

Was ordered to take command of the regiment (being the oldest captain) which at this time was very much reduced by the many & repeated actions with the enemy, & hardships & many privations endured. The [rifle] regiment in the course of the insuing spring was engaged in frequent skirmishing on the enemies lines.[69]

The advent of spring brought improved conditions for the Americans and a change in the routine of camp life, thanks largely to the efforts of a German volunteer named Friedrich Wilhelm Steuben. Steuben convinced General Washington to replace the various regional military drills of the army, which resulted in confusion on the battlefield, with a uniform system

---

[66] "General Washington to Henry Laurens, 22 December, 1777," *The Papers of George Washington, Vol. 12*, 667
[67] Posey Biography
[69] Ibid.

that all the regiments were required to use. The troops spent countless hours learning Steuben's new drill. Gradually, a more professional army developed, one that performed admirably in its first test, the battle of Monmouth.

As summer approached, rumors circulated throughout Valley Forge that the British planned to evacuate Philadelphia. The city's capture did not force the Americans to the bargaining table as was expected. In fact, in June 1778, Congress spurned British peace overtures that effectively gave America everything it demanded before 1776. Parliament renounced its right to tax, or even rule over the colonies, except on issues of trade.[70]

The lack of progress in the conflict cost General Howe his command. He returned to Britain in May to defend his actions. General Henry Clinton replaced Howe and was immediately confronted with a new strategic problem, France's entry into the conflict.

News of the alliance with France bolstered American spirits and caused the British to alter their strategy. Britain could no longer depend on complete dominance of the sea. Her other global possessions were at risk and had to be protected. This stretched British resources and drew much needed men and supplies away from America.

The British, concerned that their forces were overextended, decided to consolidate around New York. Preparations for Philadelphia's evacuation began in May. By June 18th, Clinton's army, along with thousands of loyalist civilians, were on the move. A portion of the army, and many of the loyalists, departed the city by ship. The remainder, numbering over 10,000 men, marched across New Jersey.[71]

---

[70] William Stryker, *The Battle of Monmouth*, (Princeton: Princeton Univ. Press, 1927), 35

[71] Mark M. Boatner III, *Encyclopedia of the American Revolution, 3rd. Ed.* (Stackpole Books, 1994), 716 (Originally published in 1966)

General Washington, with nearly 11,000 men, cautiously pursued the British.[72] He sent Colonel Morgan's rifle corps, bolstered to 600 men by the addition of 25 chosen marksmen from each brigade, to harass the right flank of the enemy.[73]

It is doubtful that many of Morgan's reinforcements carried rifles because the number of American riflemen in the army plummeted at Valley Forge. Enlistment expirations and attrition were two reasons for this. Another reason for the decline in the number of riflemen was a preference among many officers for muskets over rifles. General Anthony Wayne's view on rifles was shared by an increasing number of officers:

I don't like rifles – I would almost as soon face an Enemy with a good Musket and Bayonet without ammunition – as with ammunition without a bayonet; for altho' there are not many instances of bloody bayonets yet I am Confident that one bayonet keeps off an Other...The enemy knowing the Defenseless State of our Riflemen rush on – they fly –mix with or pass thro' the Other Troops and communicate fears that is ever Incident to a retiring Corps – this Would not be the Case if the Riflemen had bayonets – but it would be still better if good muskets and bayonets were put into the hands of good Marksmen and Rifles entirely laid aside. For my own part, I never wish to see one – at least without a bayonet.[74]

---

[72] "Council of War, 24 June, 1778," *The Writings of George Washington, Vol. 12,* 116

[73] "General Orders, 22 June, 1778," *The Writings of George Washington Vol. 12,* 106

[74] Charles Stille, *Major-General Anthony Wayne and the Pennsylvania Line in the Continental Army,* (Port Washington, NY : Kenniket Press, 1968), 118

(First published in 1893)

It is difficult to say exactly how many riflemen were with Washington's army in 1778. The only identifiable rifle units were two rifle companies in Lieutenant Colonel Armand's (formerly Ottendorf's) corps, and the remnants of Colonel Morgan's rifle corps. It is unclear whether riflemen continued to serve in continental regiments like the 11th Virginia. The shortage of rifles in 1777 suggests that many riflemen were converted to musket-men. If the Virginia regiments still included riflemen in 1778, they may have fought as line troops. It is more likely, however, that the riflemen exchanged their rifles for muskets, and that Colonel Morgan's and Colonel Armand's rifle troops were the only ones left in Washington's army.

While Morgan's reinforced corps hung on the right flank of the British column, General Washington sent three other large detachments forward to pressure General Clinton's rearguard.

These advance detachments engaged the British on June 28th, near Monmouth Court House. A day long battle in one hundred degree heat ensued and resulted in scores of dead. Colonel Morgan's rifle corps sat on Clinton's flank and heard the fight, but they missed the battle because of a series of miscommunications. The day ended in stalemate, with both sides still on the field. The British viewed the affair as a successful rear guard action to protect their baggage train. The Americans countered that they held their ground and inflicted heavy losses on the British. Furthermore, General Clinton's late night withdrawal to Sandy Hook left the Americans in sole possession of the field at sunrise. This rare occurrence infused the American army with pride.

Monmouth was the last major battle in the north. General Clinton concentrated his forces around New York and re-evaluated his strategy. Washington positioned his army near White Plains, New York, about 25 miles north of the city and waited for Clinton's next move.

Chapter Seven

New York Frontier

The curtailment of British military operations in 1778 gave General Washington another opportunity to reorganize his army. In early July he ordered the reinforcements attached to Colonel Morgan's corps to return to their brigades. He also consolidated many of the battle worn musket regiments. The rifle corps, depleted by casualties, illness, transfers, and enlistment expirations, was reduced to approximately one hundred men.[1] This was too few for an officer of Morgan's rank to command, yet General Washington showed no inclination to rebuild the unit.

It is possible that rifle troops fell out of favor with Washington, replaced by a desire to create a more structured light infantry corps modeled on the British. With the establishment of a formal light infantry unit still a year away, however, General Washington settled for an ad hoc force for the rest of 1778. On August 8th, Washington gave the following order:

> For the Safety and Ease of the Army and to be in greater readiness to attack or repel the Enemy, The Commander in Chief...directs that a Corps of Light Infantry composed of the best, most hardy and active Marksmen and commanded by good Partizan Officers be draughted from the several Brigades...[2]

---

[1] Richard B. LaCrosse Jr., *Revolutionary Rangers: Daniel Morgan's Riflemen and Their Role on the Northern Frontier*, (Bowie, MD: Heritage Books, 2002), 21

[2] John C. Fitzpatrick, ed., "General Orders, 8 August, 1778," *The Writings of George Washington, Vol. 12*, (U.S. Govt. Printing Officer, 1934), 300

General Charles Scott of Virginia was selected to command the light troops. Washington briefed General Scott about his expectations of the light corps:

> *With the detachment of light troops under your command you are to take post in front of our camp and in such a position as may appear best calculated to preserve the security of our own corps and cover this army from surprise...you will make yourself master of all the roads leading to the enemy's lines. You will keep in constant succession of scouting parties as large as can possibly be spared from the detachment without harassing it by too much duty. These parties are to penetrate as near the enemy's lines as possible and to continue within observing distance at all times...They will move...under circumstances the least liable to excite attention, and be careful not to kindle fires in the night, as these might betray their situation. These parties will make you, constant reports of their discoveries, and you will give me the earliest and fullest intelligence of all occurrences worthy of notice.[3]*

Washington assigned a detachment of dragoons to the light corps to aid General Scott in his mission.[4]

Scott and his light troops had a busy fall with frequent skirmishes outside of New York. Little came of these engagements, however, and when winter arrived Washington disbanded the light corps and sent the men back to their original regiments.

---

[3] "General Washington to Brigadier General Charles Scott, 14 August, 1778," *The Writings of George Washington, Vol. 12,* 323

[4] "General Orders, 14 August, 1778," *The Writings of George Washington, Vol. 12,* 324

Posey's Rifle Detachment

The establishment of Scott's Light Infantry Corps did not mean the end of rifle troops in Washington's army. Although the number and role of riflemen greatly diminished, riflemen still served an important function. Their service, however, was without the leadership of Colonel Daniel Morgan. He left the rifle corps after the battle of Monmouth, and assumed command of the combined 11th and 15th Virginia Regiments.[5]

Command of the rifle corps fell to Captain Thomas Posey. Posey was a veteran of Saratoga and had commanded the rifle corps over the winter at Valley Forge while Morgan was on furlough. Most of those riflemen, including the bulk of Posey's original company, left the rifle corps at Valley Forge when their enlistments expired. All that remained was a company of Pennsylvanians under Captain Thomas Parr and a company of Virginians under Captain Gabriel Long. Together they numbered just over a hundred men.[6]

In mid July, disturbing reports of Indian and Tory raids on the New York frontier prompted Washington to attach the rifle corps to Lieutenant Colonel William Butler's 4th Pennsylvania Regiment and send them to the region to assist. Washington informed Congress of his decision:

> *The accounts from the Western frontiers of Tyron County are distressing. The spirit of the Savages seems to be roused, and they appear determined on mischief and havoc, in every Quarter...I have detached the 4th Pennsylvania Regiment and the remains of Morgans corps* [all] *under Lt. Colo.* [William] *Butler...*

[5] Lesser, "Monthly Return of the Army...August 29, 1778," 80
[6] "Return of the Rifle Corps Under Captain Thomas Posey, 28 July, 1778," *Public Papers of George Clinton: First Governor of New York, Vol. 3,* (Albany: State Printer, 1900), 588

New York Frontier

Adapted by Lena Assad

164

to co-operate with the Militia and check the Indians if possible. [7]

Captain Posey and the rifle detachment arrived in Albany, New York on July 27[8]. They continued on to Fort Defiance in the Schoharie Valley, where Lieutenant Colonel Butler established his headquarters. Butler was eager to launch an offensive against the Indians, but a number of obstacles prevented this. Colonel Butler complained to Governor George Clinton in mid-August that,

> *I have been Obliged to Act totally on the Defensive; the little dependence that can be put in the few militia that do turn out, the disaffection of most of the Inhabitants to us, the distance and Wilderness of Country that we have to pass thro to the Enemy without the Necessaries for such an expedition, makes it very difficult in my present situation to act otherwise.* [9]

The obstacles cited by Butler delayed his offensive against the Indians until the fall. In early October, he finally set off with the 4th Pennsylvania Regiment, a detachment of Posey's riflemen, and some local militia on a two week expedition to destroy the Indian towns of Onoquaga and Unadilla.[10] The Americans arrived at Onoquaga on October 8th and destroyed the town and crops with little resistance. They moved on to

---

[7] "General Washington to Congress, 22 July, 1778," *The Writings of George Washington, Vol. 12,* 214

[8] "Colonel William Butler to Governor Clinton, 18 July, 1778," *Public Papers of George Clinton, Vol. 3,* 595

[9] "Colonel William Butler to Governor George Clinton, 13 August, 1778," *The Public Papers of George Clinton, First Governor of New York, Vol. 3,* 630-31

[10] "Extracts from Lt. Col. Butler's Journal," *Public Papers of George Clinton, Vol. 4,* 224

Unadilla, which met a similar fate, and returned to Scholarie by mid October. Although little blood was shed (largely because most of the Indian warriors were away on their own raid), Butler believed he had dealt a severe blow to the Indians and confidently informed Governor Clinton that,

> *I am well convinced that* [the expedition] *has sufficiently secured these Frontiers from any further disturbances from the Savages at least this Winter; and it will ever, hereafter,* [be] *difficult for them to distress these parts, By reason of their having no Settlements near.* [11]

Although the destruction of Onoquoga and Unadilla did create significant hardship for the Indians in the area, it did not end the fighting. In November, Joseph Brant, a Mohawk chief, led hundreds of Indians into Cherry Valley, New York to retaliate. Brant was joined by Captain Walter Butler's Tory rangers. This combined force attacked Colonel Ichabod Alden and his Massachusetts continentals early in the morning of November 10th. Alden ignored warnings of an impending attack and was killed, along with a number of soldiers and civilians. Brant was unable to capture the fort, but his men plundered and burnt the town to the ground.[12] With winter approaching the Americans had to postpone their response until the spring. Both sides settled into winter quarters.

On December 20th, General Washington ordered Thomas Posey to rejoin his regiment, the 7th Virginia. Washington also expressed his desire that the rifle corps be disbanded and the men returned to their regiments.[13] He left the final

---

[11] "Willim Butler to George Clinton, 28 October, 1778," Public Papers of George Clinton, Vol. 4, 223

[12] Max M. Mintz, *Seeds of Empire: The American Revolutionary Conquest of the Iroquois*, (New York: New York University Press, 1999), 73

[13] "General Washington to Thomas Posey, 20 December, 1778," *The Writings of George Washington, Vol. 13*, 439

decision on that matter to General James Clinton, who decided that he could not dispense with the rifle corps, so the riflemen remained at Fort Defiance.

Major Thomas Parr assumed command of the unit. Like his predecessor, Parr was an experienced soldier and fine leader. The riflemen passed a peaceful winter under Parr's command and entered spring with roughly the same number of men, around one hundred, fit for duty.[14]

Warm weather allowed the Americans to launch punitive raids against the Onondaga Indians in April. Some of Major Parr's riflemen participated in these engagements, which resulted in the total destruction of the Onondaga towns.[15] The raids were only a precursor to a much larger expedition that General Washington authorized in May 1779. He hoped that the use of overwhelming force would finally quell the unrest on the frontier.

Sullivan's Expedition

General Washington's instructions to General Sullivan were explicit:

> The expedition you are appointed to command is to be directed against the hostile tribes of the six nations of Indians...The immediate objects are the total destruction and devastation of their settlements and the capture of as many prisoners of every age and sex as possible...Parties should be detached to lay waste on all the settlements around...that the country may not be merely overrun but destroyed...You will not by any means, listen to any overture of peace before the total ruin of their settlements is effected. It is likely enough their fears

---

[14] LaCrosse, 38
[15] Ibid. 42

*if they are unable to oppose us, will compel them to
offers of peace, or policy may lead them to endeavour
to amuse us in this way to gain time and succour for
more effectual opposition. Our future security will be
in their inability to injure us; [the distance to wch.
they are driven] and in the terror with which the
severity of the chastisement they receive will inspire
them. Peace without this would be fallacious and
temporary.* [16]

General Sullivan was to destroy the ability of the natives to
wage war and in doing so, pacify the long troubled frontier.

Sullivan's expedition began as two different detachments.
General James Clinton led 1,500 men, including Major Parr's
riflemen, southwest from Conojoharie, New York to unite
with General Sullivan's 2,500 continental troops. [17] Sullivan
began his march from Easton, Pennsylvania and proceeded
through the Wyoming Valley to rendezvous with Clinton at
Tioga, along the New York – Pennsylvania border. From
there, the expedition would continue into the heart of Iroquois
County and spread as much destruction as possible. [18]

General Clinton began his march in June and slowly led his
column southwest. Major Parr's riflemen screened the
detachment from ambush with numerous scouting parties.
Clinton's advance was hampered by an abundance of supplies.
The transport of these supplies delayed his rendezvous with
General Sullivan until August. When the two detachments
finally united, General Sullivan assumed overall command
and placed Major Parr's riflemen under General Edward
Hand, the commander of Sullivan's advance guard. The
combined force marched deeper into Indian territory with the

---

[16] "General Washington to General John Sullivan, 31 May, 1778," *The
Writings of George Washington, Vol. 15,* 189

[17] Boatner, 1072

[18] "General Washington to General John Sullivan, 31 May, 1778," *The
Writings of George Washington, Vol. 15,* 189

riflemen in the lead. In late August, a party of riflemen discovered a large enemy force laying in ambush near New Town, New York. It was Joseph Brant with approximately 800 Indians and John Butler with another 250 Tories.[19]

The riflemen's discovery saved Sullivan's army from a trap and allowed General Sullivan to stage a surprise of his own. He hoped to hold the enemy in place with his artillery and General Hand's advance troops, while other units moved around Brant's flanks and encircled his force. General James Clinton described the plan to his brother:

> *About ten O' clock a scattering Fire commenced between some of their Scouts and a few of our Rifle men & Volunteers when the former gave way, and the latter proceeded until they plainly discouvered their Works which were very extensive, tho' not impregnable. As our design was not to drive them, but to surround or bring them to a fair open action...it was concluded that the artillery supported by Genl. Hand with the Infantry and Rifle Corps shoud commence the action...allowing sufficient time for General Poor's and my brigade to gain their right Flank, while Maxwell's and the covering party under Col. Ogden might gain their left.[20]*

Unfortunately for the Americans, the flanking parties were delayed by difficult terrain. Brant and Butler grew suspicious and fled before the trap closed. General James Clinton noted,

---

[19] Boatner, 794

[20] "James Clinton to His Brother, 30 August, 1779," *Papers of George Clinton, Vol. 5,* 225-226

About one O' clock Col. Proctor commenced a very warm Cannonade upon their Works, which continued near two hours...The Enemy finding their Situation in their Lines rather uncomfortable and finding we did not intend to storm them, abandoned them... [21]

Lieutenant Erkuries Beatty of Colonel Butler's 4th Pennsylvania, provided a more detailed account of the battle in his journal:

We found the Enemy strongly Entrenched with Logs, Dirt brush &ct the firing Imidiately begun in front with the Rifle Corps & the Indians made great halooing, orders were given then for the troops to form in line of battle which was done. Genl. Hands brigade in front but none of the troops advanced as we discovered the main body of the Enemy was here and had their front secured by a large Morass & brook, their right by the River & on their left partly in the rear was a very large hill, their lines extended upwards of a Mile the firing was kept up very briskly by the Rifle men & a company who was sent to reinforce them, likewise the Indians returned the fire very brisk with many shouts for about 2 hours while a disposition was made to attack them.

Genl. Clintons & Poors brigades were sent off round their left flank to take possession of the hill in the Enemys rear and extend their line intirely round them if possible. After they had gone about half an hour Genl. Hands brigade advanced in a line of battle with all our Artillery in the Centre within about 300 Yards of the Enemys works but in full View of them a very heavy cannonade began & throwing of Shells the enemy returned the fire very briskly for about half an hour when the Enemy retreated up the

---

[21] Ibid.

hill in a great Disorder & as they got near the top received a very heavy fire from Genl. Poor's brigade: the enemy then took around Genl. Poors right flank by the river which Genl. Poors had not guarded as he had not the time to, therefore they made their Escape leaving a number of their dead behind them. As soon as the Enemy left their works Genl. Hands brigade pursued them up the hill as far as where Genl. Poor was when we make a halt, the rifle men pursued them about one Mile farther....[22]

The withdrawal of Brant and Butler exposed the region to Sullivan's wrath. Over the next month, forty Indian towns were burned and thousands of bushels of food destroyed. Worst of all was the destruction of nearly every fruit orchard in the region, something that took decades to restore.[23]

The destruction caused by the Americans came at a price to the riflemen. Two weeks after the battle of Newtown, Lieutenant Thomas Boyd led a small detachment of riflemen on a patrol and fell into an Indian ambush. Most of his men were killed in the fight. Lieutenant Boyd was not so fortunate. He was captured and brutally tortured to death.[24]

The demise of Boyd's patrol was the largest American loss of the expedition. After a month long rampage, the Americans left the shattered frontier. General Clinton led his detachment back to New York, and General Sullivan returned with his men to Washington's army. Major Parr's riflemen remained with General Sullivan's force and marched to Pompton, New Jersey and then West Point.[26] General Washington decided to

---

[22] Frederick Cook, ed., "Journal of Lieut. Erkuries Beatty", *Journals of the Military Expedition of Major General John Sullivan Against the Six Nations of Indians in 1779*, (Freeport, NY: Books for Library Press, 1887), 26-27
[23] Boatner, 1076 ; See also, LaCrosse, 67-68
[24] LaCrosse, 61-67
[26] LaCrosse, 68

171

disband the rifle detachment and send the men back to their original units. The order was issued on November 7th, 1779:

> *The officers and privates composing the rifle corps under the command of Major Parr, are all to join their respective regiments. The Major will see that all the rifles and their proper bullet moulds &c., are collected and numbered to prevent their being mixed or seperated, and have them then delivered to the Commissary of Military Stores and take his receipt for the same. The Commissary is to cause the rifles &c. to be carefully boxed up and is not to deliver any of them without an order from the Commander in Chief. Muskets are to be drawn for the men in lieu of the rifles. The General cannot dissolve this corps without offering his particular thanks to the officers and soldiers remaining in it for their long, faithful and important services.*[27]

The dissolution of the rifle corps marked the temporary end of rifle troops in Washington's army. This was not necessarily a sign of displeasure from General Washington, but rather the standard procedure for most detached units in the winter. General Anthony Wayne's light infantry corps, which was formed in the summer and performed brilliantly at Stony Point, was also disbanded for the winter. Like the riflemen, the light troops joined their original regiments.

For the Virginia riflemen of Parr's Corps, it was the end of combat in the north. General Washington sent the entire Virginia line to South Carolina in December to assist with the defense of Charleston. The riflemen that remained with Washington were all Pennsylvanians.

---

[27] " General Orders, 7 November, 1779," *The Writings of George Washington from the Original Manuscript Sources, 1745-1799.* (Online thru the Library of Congress)

Parr's Rifle Corps Is Re-formed

General Washington decided to reconstitute the rifle detachment in 1780. On July 26th, he ordered

> The 1st and 3rd Pennsylvania regiments [to] furnish a company of riflemen each of forty two rank and file. If these regiments have not the number of riflemen requisite the deficiency is to be drawn from the other regiments of that line and the aforemention'd regiments will furnish an equal number of men to the others in Exchange. Major Parr will take command of these two Companies and will take immediate measures for preparing Arms and Acoutrements.[28]

It quickly became apparent that raising eighty riflemen strained the army's capabilities. On July 27th, Washington cut the allotment of men from the 1st and 3rd Pennsylvania regiments in half:

> The Two rifle companies directed to be formed in the order of yesterday will for the present only consist of twenty rank and file pr Company, they are to be completed to forty two from the Levies who are fit for this Service, as fast as they arrive...[29]

Parr's rifle detachment was eventually outfitted, but it, along with the rest of Washington's army, remained relatively inactive in 1780. The focus of the war shifted south, and other riflemen were destined to play a crucial role in the struggle there.

---

[28] "General Orders, 26 July, 1780," *The Writings of George Washington, Vol. 19,* 252

[29] General Orders, 27 July, 1780," *The Writings of George Washington, Vol. 19,* 263

Chapter Eight

Rifles in the South

Thousands of southern soldiers, including many riflemen, fought under General Washington in the north. Thousands more remained home and served in their local militia. The militia forces of Georgia, the Carolinas, and Virginia were often a mixture of musket-men and riflemen. In the western region of these states, rifles vastly outnumbered muskets.

Numerous engagements between frontier riflemen and Indian/Tory war parties occurred in the west. The legendary Daniel Boone was one rifleman who fought there. George Rogers Clark was another. In 1778, Clark led nearly 200 riflemen on an epic march deep into the frontier to secure the western territory from the British.[1]

Riflemen also played an important role in the southern campaign. They harassed British work parties at Charleston and fought throughout South Carolina in partisan units under Francis Marion, Charles Sumter, and Andrew Pickens. The single biggest impact of southern riflemen, however, came in October 1780 at King's Mountain.

King's Mountain

On the evening of October 6th, 1780, nine hundred mounted riflemen from the backwoods of Virginia and the Carolinas left Cowpens, South Carolina. They were chasing Major Patrick Ferguson and his 1,100 Loyalist troops. A month earlier Ferguson threatened to march into the frontier and punish disloyal subjects of the crown. Instead of intimidating the frontiersmen, however, Ferguson provoked them.

---

[1] Boatner, 1190

175

Colonel William Campbell led two hundred Virginians to South Carolina and joined riflemen under Colonels Thomas Brandon, William Hill, and Edward Lacy. Hundreds of North Carolina riflemen under Colonels Isaac Shelby, John Sevier, Benjamin Cleveland, and Joseph McDowell also marched to Cowpens.[2] The officers placed Colonel Campbell in charge of the loose detachment and rode east to pay Major Ferguson a visit.

Ferguson knew that the riflemen were coming and appealed to area loyalists to join him:

> *Gentlemen: -- Unless you wish to be eat up by an inundation of barbarians, who have begun by murdering an unarmed son before their aged father, and afterwards lopped off his arms, and who by their shocking cruelties and irregularities, give the best proof of their cowardice and want of discipline; I say, if you wish to be pinioned, robbed, and murdered, and see your wives and daughters, in four days, abused by the dregs of mankind – in short, if you wish or deserve to live, and bear the name of men, grasp your arms in a moment and run to camp.*[3]

The tone of the letter conveyed Ferguson's disdain for the riflemen, yet a dispatch to General Cornwallis dated October 6th, hinted of his concern:

> *My Lord:* [The riflemen have] *become an object of some consequence. Happily their leaders are obliged to feed their followers with such hopes, and so to flatter them with accounts of our weakness and fear, that, if necessary, I should hope for success against*

[2] Patrick O' Kelly, *Nothing but Blood and Slaughter: The Revolutionary War in the Carolinas, Vol. 2*, 322-325

[3] Lyman C. Draper, *King's Mountain and Its Heroes: History of the Battle of King's Mountain*, (Cincinnati : Peter G. Thomson, 1881), 204

them myself; but numbers compared, that must be doubtful. I am on my march towards you.... Three or four hundred good soldiers, part dragoons, would finish the business. Something must be done soon. This is their last push in this quarter.[4]

Sometime after Ferguson sent the dispatch, he decided to make a stand at King's Mountain and await reinforcements. Long before Cornwallis sent assistance, however, events made reinforcement unnecessary.

Major Ferguson had approximately one thousand loyalist militia from the Carolinas, of which two hundred were away foraging for supplies. He also had about a hundred Provincial troops from New Jersey and New York. The Provincials were well trained and supplied and were equal to many British regulars.[5]

Ferguson placed his men on a steep ridge approximately sixty feet high and 600 yards long. It varied in width from 60 to 200 yards and was shaped like a foot, with the narrow portion, or heel, running southwest of the wider portion, or toes. There was little cover on the crest as it was devoid of trees or brush. The sides of the ridge and the surrounding area were wooded, however, and provided cover for the Americans. The riflemen arrived in the afternoon of October 7th. They were tired, wet, and hungry after an all night ride in the rain. Colonel Isaac Shelby recalled,

When the patriots came near the mountain they halted, tied all their loose baggage to their saddles, fastened their horses, and left them under charge of a few men, and then prepared for an immediate attack. About three o'clock the patriot force was led to the attack in four columns – Col. Campbell commanded

---

[4] Draper, 206-207
[5] Boatner, 579

*the right center column, Col. Shelby the left center,
Col. Sevier the right flank column, and Col.
Cleveland the left flank. As they came to the foot of
the mountain the right center and right flank columns
deployed to the right, and the left center and left flank
columns to the left....*[6]

Colonel William Campbell described the initial phase of the
battle:

*Col. Shelby's regiment and mine began the attack,
and sustained the whole fire of the enemy for about
ten minutes, while the other troops were forming
around the height upon which the enemy were posted.
The firing then became general, and as heavy as you
can conceive for the number of men. The
advantageous situation of the enemy, being the top of
a steep ridge, obliged us to expose ourselves
exceedingly; and the dislodging of them was almost
equal to driving men from strong breast-works.*[7]

Colonel Campbell urged his men forward shouting, *"Here they
are, my brave boys, shout like hell, and fight like devils!"*[8]
The Virginians scurried up the steep slope using trees and
boulders for cover. As they approached the crest, Major
Ferguson ordered a bayonet charge to push them back. The
Virginians, lacking bayonets, fled down the hill where Colonel
Campbell rallied them. The Tories returned to the crest and
turned their attention to Colonel Shelby's North Carolinians.
Shelby's men were opposite Campbell's, and were about to

---

[6] Draper, "Colonel Isaac Shelby's Account of King's Mountain," 543
[7] Draper, "Col. Wm. Campbell to Col. Arthur Campbell, 20 October,
1780," 526
[8] Draper, 247

reach the crest, when they too were pushed back by a bayonet charge. Shelby recalled years later that,

> *As [the riflemen] would approach the summit, Ferguson would order a charge with fixed bayonet, which was always successful, for the riflemen retreated before the charging column slowly, still firing as they retired.* [9]

The fight intensified as the rest of the riflemen joined the battle. James Collins, an American rifleman from South Carolina, recalled,

> *We were soon in motion, every man throwing four or five balls in his mouth to prevent thirst, also to be in readiness to reload quick. The shot of the enemy soon began to pass over us like hail...We soon attempted to climb the hill, but were fiercely charged upon and forced to fall back to our first position; we tried a second time, but met the same fate; the fight seemed to become more furious.* [10]

Another rifleman, John Henry of North Carolina, fell victim to one of Ferguson's bayonet charges. He recalled,

> *We...advanced up the hill close to the Tory lines. There was a log across a hollow that I took my stand by, and stepping one step back, I was safe from the British fire. I there remained firing until the British charged bayonet. When they made the charge they first fired their guns...I was preparing to fire when*

---

[9] Draper, "Colonel Isaac Shelby's Account of King's Mountain," 543
[10] John M. Roberts, ed., *Autobiography of a Revolutionary Soldier*, (New York : Arno Press, 1979), 52
(Originally published in 1859)

one of the advancing British...gave me a thrust
through my hand and into my thigh.[11]

Ferguson's men chased Henry's comrades to the bottom of the hill and then returned to the crest to repeat the process. Time and again Ferguson's troops forced the riflemen back, but only temporarily. Most of them rallied to their officers at the base of the hill and resumed the attack. Colonel Shelby noted,

> *When Ferguson's men returned to regain their*
> *position on the mountain, the patriots would again*
> *rally and pursue them. In one of these charges,*
> *Shelby's column was considerably broken; he rode*
> *back and rallied his men, and when the enemy retired*
> *to the summit, he pressed on his men and reached the*
> *summit whilst Ferguson was directing a charge*
> *against [Col.] Cleveland.* [12]

The entire hill was ablaze with gunfire and shrouded with smoke as the riflemen converged on the crest. Communication and coordination was difficult for both sides, but especially for the Americans who were spread out. Many overcame this by following the advice of Colonel Cleveland:

> *Every man must consider himself an officer, and act*
> *from his own judgment. Fire as quick as you can,*
> *and stand your ground as long as you can. When*
> *you can do no better, get behind trees, or retreat; but*
> *I beg you not quite to run off. If we are repulsed, let*
> *us make a point of returning, and renewing the*
> *fight....*[13]

---

[11] "Kings Mountain Expedition," *An Annual Publication of Historical Papers: Governor W.W. Holden and Revolutionary Documents, Series 3,* (Durham, NC : Historical Society of Trinity College, 1899), 85
[12] Ibid.
[13] Draper, 249

Largely on their own initiative, the riflemen maintained constant pressure on the Tories. Thomas Young recalled,

> *Ben Hollingsworth and myself took right up the side of the mountain, and fought from tree to tree... to the summit. I recollect I stood behind one tree and fired until the bark was nearly knocked off, and my eyes pretty well filled with it....*[14]

As the riflemen reached the crest, Ferguson's situation grew increasingly desperate. Alexander Chesney, a local Tory fighting with Ferguson, noted,

> *The Americans who had been repulsed had regained their former stations and sheltered behind trees poured in an irregular destructive fire; in this manner the engagement was maintained near an hour, the mountaniers flying whenever there was danger of being charged by the Bayonet, and returning again so soon as the British detachment had faced about to repel another of their parties.*[15]

Ferguson's reliance on the bayonet, coupled with the riflemen's deadly fire upon his exposed men, meant that the Tories suffered heavy casualties. A few Tories attempted to surrender, which provoked an angry response from their commander. One observer heard Ferguson exclaim that, "*He never would yield to such damned banditti.*"[16] Shortly after he made this statement, Ferguson was dead, shot from his horse by a number of riflemen. Command of the Tories fell to Captain DePeyser, who quickly surrendered. The riflemen

---

[14] George Scheer and Hugh *Rankin, Rebels and Redcoats,* 418
[15] E. Alfred Jones, ed., *The Journal of Alexander Chesney, A South Carolina Loyalist in the Revolution and After,* (Printed from a copy of the Ohio State Library, 1921), 17-18
[16] Draper, 543

were slow to give quarter, and many unfortunate Tories fell before the firing ceased.

The battle of King's Mountain was a huge victory for the Americans. Coming on the heels of major defeats at Charleston and Camden, the success at King's Mountain significantly boosted American morale. It also caused General Cornwallis to suspend his march into North Carolina until the situation in South Carolina stabilized.

General Horatio Gates, the commander of American forces in the south, was thrilled by the victory and wrote to Governor Thomas Jefferson of Virginia that, *"We are now more than even with the Enemy."*[17] The victory took some of the sting out of his disastrous defeat at Camden two months earlier, a defeat that ultimately cost Gates his command in December when he was replaced by General Nathanael Greene.

Greene inherited an army that had largely recovered from Camden but was still unable to stand against General Cornwallis in the Carolinas. Greene's best troops were his Maryland and Delaware continentals. They were augmented by hundreds of militia and about one hundred cavalry. Although the victory at Kings Mountain bolstered morale, the army remained in poor condition. General Greene complained that,

> *The appearance of the troops was wretched beyond description, and their distress, on account of* [lack of] *provisions, was little less than their suffering for want of clothing and other necessities.*[18]

---

[17] Julian P. Boyd, "Horatio Gates to Thomas Jefferson, 12 October, 1780," *The Papers of Thomas Jefferson, Vol. 4*, (Princeton, NJ : Princeton University Press, 1951), 32

[18] "Nathanael Greene to Thomas Jefferson, 6 December," 1780, *The Papers of Thomas Jefferson, Vol. 4*, 183

General Greene addressed the army's supply needs by dividing his force -- moving the main body to Cheraw Hill, South Carolina. This placed them further away from Cornwallis, who was in Winnsboro, South Carolina. To counter the appearance that he was retreating, Greene sent General Daniel Morgan with 600 of his best troops in the opposite direction to threaten British outposts in South Carolina's interior.

Morgan had only recently returned to the army in October after a self imposed hiatus. He left in dusgust in 1779 because he had been passed over for command of Washington's new light infantry corps. The command went to General Anthony Wayne, who validated his selection with his performance at Stony Point. After the American defeat at Camden, however, Morgan returned to the army as a newly promoted Brigadier General. He took command of the southern army's light infantry troops, which included 400 continentals, two companies of Virginia militia, and nearly 100 light dragoons.[19]

On December 21st, Morgan led his light corps west to link up with militia troops and threaten the British outpost at Ninety-Six. By Christmas, over one hundred miles separated Morgan and Greene.

---

[19] Lee, *The Revolutionary War Memoirs of General Henry Lee*, (New York : Da Capo Press, 1998), 222
(Originally published in 1812)

South Carolina

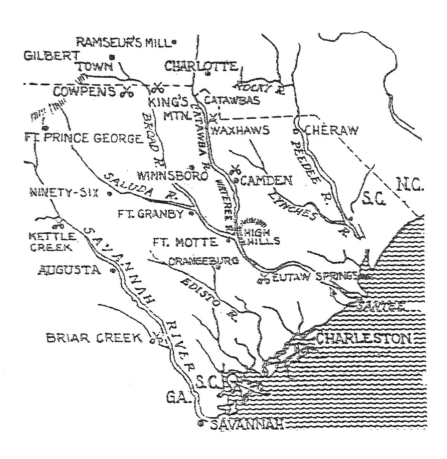

Adapted by Lena Assad

General Cornwallis, concerned about Ninety-Six, sent Colonel Banastre Tarleton to reinforce it. Tarleton positioned his legion between Morgan and the outpost and soon realized that Morgan was not coming. Never one to avoid a fight, Tarleton proposed that Cornwallis position his army to block Morgan's route back to General Greene, while he [Tarleton] pushed Morgan northeast towards Cornwallis:

> *When I advance* [north toward Morgan] *I must either destroy Morgan's corps, or push it before me over Broad river, towards King's mountain. The advance of the army* [under Cornwallis] *should commence ... onwards for King's mountain.*[20]

Tarleton hoped to trap Morgan between two strong British forces and annihilate him. General Cornwallis agreed with Tarleton's proposal and both marched north.

Morgan was aware of the coordinated movements against him but displayed little concern. He expected militia reinforcements and held his position at Grindall's Shoals. Morgan intended to engage Tarleton at the Pacolet River crossings. On January 14th, however, Tarleton unexpectedly crossed the river below the Americans and forced General Morgan to retreat.

Aware of the threat Cornwallis posed to the east, Morgan withdrew to the northwest. This drew Tarleton away from Cornwallis and Morgan away from the trap. The Americans halted at Cowpens, just a few miles south of the Broad River. Morgan assessed the terrain and his force, which slowly grew with the arrival of more militia, and resolved to make a stand.

---

[20] Lieut. Col. Banastre Tarleton, " Tarleton to Earl Cornwallis, 4 January, 1781," *A History of the Campaigns of 1780 and 1781 in the Southern Provinces of North America*, (North Stratford, NH : Ayer Company Publishers, 1999), 246
(Originally published in 1787)

The Battle of Cowpens

General Morgan spent the evening of January 16th, preparing his men for battle. One soldier recalled,

> *It was upon this occasion I was more perfectly convinced of Gen. Morgan's qualifications to command militia, than I had ever before been. He went among the volunteers, helped them fix their swords, joked with them about their sweet-hearts, told them to keep in good spirits, and the day would be ours. And long after I laid down, he was going about among the soldiers encouraging them, and telling them that the old wagoner would crack his whip over Ben. [Tarleton] in the morning, as sure as they lived. 'Just hold up your heads, boys, three fires,' he would say, ' and you are free, and then when you return to your homes, how the old folks will bless you, and the girls kiss you, for your gallant conduct!' I don't believe he slept a wink that night!*[21]

Morgan's experience told him not to rely too heavily on the militia and he developed a battle plan accordingly. It called for a defense in depth comprising three battle lines. Morgan placed approximately 150 militia riflemen from Georgia and the Carolinas in a skirmish line that extended across the road that Tarleton was expected to approach from.[22] They deployed in loose order behind trees and were ordered to *"feel the enemy as he approached."*[23] Since they were ordered to hold their fire until the enemy was within fifty yards, the riflemen were only expected to fire a shot or two before

---

[21] Scheer and Rankin, " Thomas Young", 428
[22] Boatner, 293
[23] Lawrence E. Babits, *A Devil of a Whipping: The Battle of Cowpens*, (Chapel Hill : The University of North Carolina Press, 1998), 81

withdrawing to the flanks of the next American line 150 yards in their rear.[24]

Morgan's second line consisted of 300 North and South Carolina militia, many armed with rifles.[25] It also stretched across the road and was divided into four battalions. Unlike the skirmishers, who fired individually, the militia line fired massed battalion volleys. General Morgan expected each battalion to fire at least two volleys before they retreated to the third and final American line.

Morgan's third line consisted of his best troops, the Maryland, Delaware, and Virginia continentals. They were augmented by two companies of Virginia militia -- many with rifles -- a company of Virginia State troops, and a few North Carolina militia and state troops. The line was formed in two ranks about 150 yards behind the militia and numbered about 550.[26]

Lieutenant Colonel William Washington commanded about 120 cavalry troops: two thirds continental and the rest mounted militia.[27] They were held in reserve behind the third line. A few horsemen were posted three miles ahead of the skirmish line as pickets.

Colonel Tarleton advanced towards Cowpens early in the morning of January 17th. He commanded approximately 1,100

---

[24] Ibid

[25] Boatner, 293

Note: The number of troops in the militia line has been reported as high as 1,000. See Tarleton, 216; If the bulk of the skirmish line joined the militia line then the number would have approached 500 at the very least.

[26] Exact figures for this line, as for the entire American force, vary widely. The number above is an approximation based on the literature on Cowpens.

[27] Babits, 41-42

Cowpens

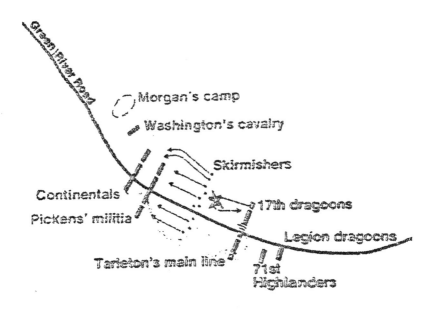

Adapted by Lena Assad

188

men, including over 300 cavalry and 750 infantry troops. Tarleton also had 2 three pound artillery pieces.[28]

Tarleton's force confronted Morgan's pickets before sunrise and pressed forward, reaching Cowpens at dawn. The Americans were deployed and waiting for him. Thomas Young, attached to Washington's cavalry, recalled,

> *The morning...was bitterly cold...About sunrise, the British line advanced at a sort of trot with a loud halloo. It was the most beautiful line I ever saw. When they shouted, I heard Morgan say, 'They give us the British halloo, boys. Give them the Indian halloo, by G--!' and he galloped along the lines, cheering the men and telling them not to fire until we could see the whites of their eyes.*[29]

The American skirmish line hampered Colonel Tarleton's ability to see Morgan's troop disposition, so he ordered some dragoons forward to drive the riflemen back. The horsemen advanced towards the line and were met by a scattered, but deadly fire. The riflemen, secure behind trees, did not budge, and it was the dragoons that were driven back.

Colonel Tarleton grew impatient and attacked. His troops dropped their extra gear and formed battle lines across the road. As they advanced in open order towards the American skirmish line, Morgan's riflemen peppered them with *"a heavy & galling fire."*[30] A few inexperienced British soldiers responded with unauthorized shots, but most held their fire and continued forward, driving the riflemen back to the militia line.

---

[28] John Buchanan, *The Road to Guilford Courthouse: The American Revolution in the Carolinas*, (New York : John Wiley & Sons, 1997), 321
[29] Scheer and Rankin, " Thomas Young", 430
[30] Richard K. Showman, "General Daniel Morgan to General Nathanael Greene, 19 January, 1781," *The Papers of General Nathanael Greene, Vol. 7*, (Chapel Hill : University of North Carolina Press, 1994), 154

General Morgan placed a handful of riflemen a few paces in front of the militia line to begin the action there. One of these riflemen recalled,

> *Morgan had picked out eleven of us who were to fire as a signal for opening the ball, and placed us in front several paces...When they came near enough for us to distinguish plainly their faces, we picked out our man and let fly.*[31]

Their shots precipitated a devastating fire upon the British as each militia battalion unleashed a well aimed volley into their ranks. *"The effect of the fire was considerable,"* noted one British officer, *"it produced something like a recoil."* [32] One company lost two thirds of its strength.[33] Despite the heavy fire, Tarleton's men pressed on and forced the militia to retreat before most had a chance to fire a second time. Their withdrawal was not disorderly, however. A continental officer in the third line observed that the militia,

> *Being overpowered by the superior number of the enemy...retreated, but in very good order, not seeming to be in the least confused.*[34]

They sought safety behind the third line but were shocked to find a large party of Tarleton's horsemen riding down on them. One soldier recalled,

> *Just as we got to our horses, they* [Tarleton's cavalry] *overtook us and began to take a few hacks at some...But in a few moments, Colonel Washington's*

---

[31] Babits, 90
[32] Ibid. 92
[33] Ibid.
[34] Babits, 95

cavalry was among them like a whirlwind, and the poor fellows began to keel from their horses without being able to remount. The shock was so sudden and violent they could not stand it, and immediately betook themselves to flight.[35]

The timely arrival of Washington's dragoons spared the militia and rallied their spirits. Many returned to the fight and helped decide the battle's outcome.

While Washington's cavalry routed the 17th Dragoons, Morgan's main line braced for a confrontation with Tarleton. The British briefly halted to dress and close ranks. They were well within range of Morgan's riflemen in the third line and endured a warm fire from them. The fight intensified as the British resumed their advance, and Morgan's continentals opened fire. *"When the Enemy advanced to our Line, they received a well-directed and incessant Fire,"* noted Morgan.[36] Thomas Young was especially impressed by the continental volleys:

When the regulars fired, it seemed like one sheet of flame from right to left. Oh! It was beautiful.[37]

The British responded in kind. Tarleton observed, *"The fire on both sides was well supported, and produced much slaughter."*[38] Another participant noted that both sides *"Maintained their ground with great bravery; and the conflict...was obstinate and bloody."*[39]

---

[35] Roberts, " James Collins", *Autobiography of a Revolutionary Soldier*, 57
[36] "General Daniel Morgan to General Nathanael Greene, 19 January, 1781", *The Papers of General Nathanael Greene, Vol. 7*, 154
[37] Scheer and Rankin, " Thomas Young", 430
[38] Tarleton, 216
[39] Babits, 103

Colonel Tarleton tried to break the deadlock by striking at Morgan's right flank. He recalled,

> *As the contest between the British infantry in the front line and the continentals seemed equally balanced, neither retreating,* [I] *thought the advance of the 71ˢᵗ* [battalion] *into line, and a movement of the cavalry in reserve to threaten the enemy's right flank, would put a victorious period to the action.*[40]

The right flank of the American line was held by Captain Andrew Wallace's company of Virginia continentals. Among the trees on their right, a few yards in advance of them, were North Carolina riflemen under Major Charles McDowell. These were the same riflemen who began the battle on the skirmish line. They were now delivering long range shots into Tarleton's left flank.

In order to turn the American flank, Tarleton had to go through the riflemen and around the Virginia continentals. His dragoons did this, scattering the riflemen and passing around Captain Wallace's right. Just as they were about to cause havoc in the rear, they were intercepted by Colonel Washington's cavalry and forced to retreat.

The American line was still in jeopardy, however, because British troops from the 71ˢᵗ battalion, trailing the British dragoons, flanked the Virginians. Colonel John Howard, commander of the continentals, explained what happened:

> *Seeing my right flank was exposed to the enemy, I attempted to change the front of Wallace's company. In doing this, some confusion ensued, and first a part and then the whole of the company commenced a retreat. The officers along the line seeing this and*

---

[40] Tarleton, 217

supposing that orders had been given for a retreat, faced their men about and moved off.[41]

General Morgan, upset by the unauthorized withdrawal, confronted Colonel Howard, who calmed Morgan by proclaiming that, *"Men were not beaten who retreated in that order."* Morgan described what happened next:

We retired in good Order about 50 Paces, formed, advanced on the Enemy & gave them a fortunate Volley which threw **them** *into Disorder.*[42]

In truth, Tarleton's men were disordered prior to the American volley. The initial withdrawal of the main American line prompted the British to rush forward. *"They are coming on like a mob,"* Colonel Washington told Howard, *"give them a fire and I will charge them."*[43] Colonel Howard did precisely that, ordering his men to face about. *"In a minute we had a perfect line,"* recalled Howard.[44] He continued,

The enemy were now very near us. Our men commenced a very destructive fire, which they little expected, and a few rounds occasioned great disorder in their ranks. While in this confusion, I ordered a charge with the bayonet, which order was obeyed with great alacrity.[45]

---

[41] Commager and Steele, "Lieutenant Colonel John Eager Howard's Account," *The Spirit of Seventy-Six*, 1156
[42] "General Daniel Morgan to General Nathanael Greene, 19 January, 1781," *The Papers of General Nathanael Greene, Vol. 7*, 154
[43] Babits, 117
[44] Commager and Steele, "Lieutenant Colonel John Eager Howard's Account," *The Spirit of Seventy-Six*, 1156
[45] Ibid. 1157

General Morgan applauded Colonel Howard's leadership and described the impact of the American bayonet charge:

> *Lt. Colonel Howard observing* [the enemy's disorder] *gave orders for the Line to charge Bayonets, which was done with such Address that they fled with the utmost Precipitation, leaving the Field Pieces in our Possession. We pushed our Advantage so effectually, that they never had an Opportunity of rallying.*[46]

Tarleton's defeat at Cowpens was nearly total. His detachment was shattered and he lost over 800 men (killed, wounded, or captured).[47] Only his dragoons escaped, and they did so in disgrace when they ignored Tarleton's order to assist the infantry. Cowpens, another important American victory in the south, was won with the help of hundreds of riflemen and the leadership of the greatest rifle commander in the American army, Daniel Morgan.

As the war entered its last year of serious combat, riflemen continued to perform a vital role for American troops in the south. They protected the flanks of General Greene's army at Guilford Court House and served as the vanguard of General LaFayette's army at Green Spring, Virginia. Hundreds of other riflemen fought as militia troops in the south and west. Only in the north had riflemen essentially disappeared from the American army, and in the summer of 1781 General Washington moved to change that.

---

[46] "General Daniel Morgan to General Nathanael Greene, 19 January, 1781," *The Papers of General Nathanael Greene, Vol.* 7, 154
[47] Babits, 143

Parr's Rifle Detachment

In 1781, Washington had high hopes that reinforcements from France would finally allow him to besiege New York and drive the British out. Part of Washington's siege preparation called for the use of riflemen. In late June, he wrote to Governor Joseph Reed of Pennsylvania to request that the state recruit 300 riflemen:

> *In the course of our expected operations we shall stand in need of a species of troops, which are not at present to be procured either in this Army or in any of the States to the Northward of Pennsylvania. They are expert Rifle Men.*[48]

Washington explained that the riflemen would be important in the expected siege of New York:

> *The use of these Men will be to fire into the embrazures and to drive the enemy from their parapets when our approaches are carried very near their Works. Without this can be done, our loss will be immense when we shall come within Musket Shot.*[49]

Charleston, according to Washington, demonstrated to both sides the importance of riflemen in a siege:

> *General Lincoln informs me that the enemy made use of this mode at the Siege of Charlestown, and that his Batteries were in a manner silenced, untill he opposed the same kind of troops and made it as dangerous for the enemy to shew their Men as it had*

---

[48] "General Washington to Joseph Reed, 24 June, 1781," *The Writings of George Washington, Vol. 22,* 257
[49] Ibid.

been before for him to expose his. The number which we shall want will be about three hundred, and I shall be exceedingly obliged to your Excellency, if you will endeavour to procure so many from the Frontier of Pennsylvania.... I would wish the Corps to be formed into six Companies of 50 each, under the command of a Captain and two subs, the whole to be commanded by a Major. The term of service to the 1st. day of January next....[50]

General Washington was particularly hopeful that Major Thomas Parr would agree to command the rifle corps:

If Major Parr formerly of the 7th. Penna. Regt. would engage in such a service, a better Officer could not be found for the purpose... One of the terms [of service] should be that they are to find their own Rifles, as we have none in Store. I shall be glad to hear as soon as possible what probability there will be of succeeding in this undertaking. The greater part of the Men, must be with the Army by the 1st. of Augt. or their services will be useless afterwards.[51]

A month later, Washington wrote a second letter to Governor Reed urging him to send the riflemen to camp as quickly as possible:

As this Body of Men will be exceedingly essential to our Designs, and may be very usefully employed in Detachments, I have to beg of your Excellency that you will be pleased to give Orders, that as fast as they are recruited, they may be marched off for this Camp in small Parties from twenty to thirty in a

---

[50] Ibid. 257-258
[51] Ibid. 258

Party, as they are collected, with proper Officers to conduct the Parties: in this Mode our Operations may not be delayed by waiting for the whole Corps to be completed before we receive the Benefits of their Services.[52]

That same day Washington wrote to Major Thomas Parr:

I am pleased to find...that you have accepted of the command of the Corps of Rifle Men which are to be raised in Pennsylvania and that there is a probability that the Men will be obtained. As their services are immediately wanted, you will be pleased to send them to Camp in parties from 20 to thirty under the charge of an Officer.[53]

Alas, the need for Parr's riflemen evaporated when events in Virginia drastically changed Washington's plans. Yorktown, Virginia, became Washington's target instead of New York. In August 1781, General Washington accomplished a logistical miracle when he transferred the bulk of his army from New York to Virginia and joined the French in a siege of General Cornwallis at Yorktown.

Although Washington had planned to use Major Parr's new rifle corps in a siege of New York, Parr's riflemen did not march to Virginia. Washington relied, instead, on Virginia militia riflemen under Colonel William Lewis.

The riflemen's skills were never fully employed, however, because General Cornwallis surrendered before the American and French siege lines advanced within rifle range. Land and

---

[52] "General Washington to Joseph Reed, 28 July, 1781," *The Writings of George Washington, Vol. 22,* 426
[53] "General Washington to Major Thomas Parr 28 July, 1781," *The Writings of George Washington, Vol. 22,* 427

sea based cannon, not small arms and bayonets, decided the battle of Yorktown.

Although riflemen saw little action in the last major battle of the Revolutionary War, they played a crucial role in America's long struggle to Yorktown. American riflemen shielded the army from attack and led it into battle. Riflemen served heroically at Boston, Quebec, Long Island, Harlem Heights, Fort Washington, Trenton, Princeton, Brandywine, King's Mountain, and Cowpens. They fought Indians and Tories in the west, and British soldiers and Tories in the south. They shielded the American army at Valley Forge, and American settlers on the New York frontier. Most importantly, American riflemen played a pivotal role in the battle of Saratoga, the turning point of the war. Their seven years of service proved that General Washington was right when he declared that the riflemen were, *"Indeed a Very Useful Corps."*

Appendix

An Incomplete List of Riflemen Who Served In Colonel Daniel Morgan's Rifle Corps in 1777

Pay Rolls transcribed by Joseph Craig

Captain Thomas Posey's Company

Capt.	Thomas Posey
Lt.	Adam Wallace
Lt.	J. Hobson
Lt.	John Buchanan
Lt.	John Lapsley
Sgt.	Samuel Bartran
Sgt.	Jn. Crafford
Sgt.	Wm. Chochran
Sgt.	Joseph Evins
Cpl.	Robert McNeeley
Cpl.	Jas. Sterling
Cpl.	Thomas Wilson
Cpl.	Joseph Dunkin
Cpl.	Edward Edwards
Cpl.	Benjamin Abbott
Cpl.	Jeremiah Samuel
Cpl.	Smith Kent

Jacob Price
Wm. Hanson
John Rickey
Jn. Hundley
Thomas Davice
Joseph McCalister
Joseph Anderson
Jerimiah Garison
Andrew Fares
Andrew Elder
James Maguyre
John Eagar
Wm. McNeal
Wm. Stewart
John McBride
Joshua Dean

Anthony Crockett
Samuel Burks
Andrew Crafford
Boston Dramwood
John Dunkin
Thomas Weahley
Daniel Donikan
John Sanders
John Cole
Wm. Rhea
George Fielder
Andrew Meak
Wm. Mericer
Charles Mayfield
Molisin Parigin
Richard Scaggs
James Cartright
James Blackborn
Robert Barned
John Cheatwood
Terry Galaway
Terry Northcoat
Elijah Hendrick
James Troop
William Anderson
William Hill
John Douglass
William Graham
Thomas Potter
William Terril
Johnson Tyler
Caleb Smith
John Crawdy

Captain Samuel Cabell's Company

Capt.	Samuel Cabell
Lt.	Benjamin Taliaferro
Lt.	John Stokes
Lt.	John Jordan
Lt.	Phillip Hockaday
Ens.	Robert Watkins
Sgt.	Samuel August
Sgt.	Thomas Beaufort
Sgt.	John Thomas
Sgt.	Daniel Low
Sgt.	Edward Cox
Sgt.	------ Pattison
Drum	James Weaker
Cpl.	Thomas Dickenson
Cpl.	James Hill
Cpl.	John Jones
	John Carperter
	William Montgomery
	William Johnson
	Samuel Bell
	Benjamin Galloway
	Jonah Welch
	Josiah Cheatham
	Thomas Gregory
	Daniel Taylor
	John Sherrald
	Thomas Smith
	William Brookes
	John Welch
	Austin Smith
	William Barfoot
	Osborn Coffey
	George Kay
	John Sawyer
	Thomas Johns
	William Johns

Captain Gabriel Long's Company

Capt.	Gabriel Long
Lt.	A. Tannehill
Lt.	James Harrison
Ens.	Reuben Long
Sgt.M	John Coleman
Sgt.	Nick Long
Cpl.	David Hartley
Cpl.	Anthony Garnett
	Wm. Lloyd
	Henry Holdway
	Reuben Long
	Thomas Wright
	John Thomas
	Isaac Miller
	Evans Long
	John Harrison
	B. Moore
	Jacob Smith
	Patrick Harrison

From Capt. Sheppard's Company of the 11th Virg.

	John Smith
	---- Davis
	Benjamin McKnight
	Adam Rider

From Capt. Thorn's Company of the 3rd Virg.

Cpl.	John Slaughter

From Capt. Wm. Blackwell's Company of the 11th Virg.

Sgt.	John Morgan
Cpl.	Wm. Southard
	Charles Morgan
	David Grant
	Mark Robinson
	John Shaughan
	William Dennis
	John Grant

From Capt. Alexander Lawson Smith's Company of Rawling's Regt. & the 11th Virg.

Sgt.	John Thompson
Cpl.	John Howe
	Thomas DeArmot
	John Coleman
	John Johnston
	Peter D.

From Capt. Wm. Smith's Company of the 11th Virg.

Moses Spincer

From Capt. Peter Bruin's Company of the 11th Virg.

Cpl.	John Yassaway
Cpl.	Duncan McDonald
	Peter Carland
	Wm. Liggett
	Wm. Castle
	John Meade
	Chris Roney
	David Ray
	John Smith
	John Lyon

From Capt. Charle Porterfield's Company of the 11th Virg.

Sgt.	Elias Toland
Sgt.	Soloman ???
	John Hopewell
	Abraham Grant
	Wm. Jacobs
	Daniel Davidson
	John Robinson
	Abraham Brown
	John Huston
	Chris Duncan
	John Anderson
	John Adams
	James Jiles
	Samuel Middleton

Captain Hawkins Boon's Company

Capt.	Hawkins Boon	John Casper	Isaac Prosser
Lt.	Alexander Martin	Wm. Delany	John Irwin
Sgt.	John McMachran	Sam Craig	John Teed
Sgt.	John Watson	Wm. Smith	John Curry
Sgt.	Patrick Campbell	Thomas Benson	Wm. Glover
Sgt.	Benjamin Custard	Edward Usselton	Wm. FcFeely
Cpl.	Alexander McCoy	James Murdock	Joseph Lyons
Cpl.	Benjamin Whealer	James Everingham	John McKiney
Cpl.	John Williamson	John McKreary	
	Sam Porter	Robert Shepherd	
	George Martin	Charles Sample	
	James Hamilton	John Woolabor	
	Joseph Silverthorn	Charles Mchahan	
	Daniel Armstrong	Isaac Hazelton	
	Patrick McMachan	Michael Teeter	
	Edward Lee	Thomas Fitzgerald	
	Samuel Matson	William McLan	
	Andrew Clark	Emmit Mallek	
	William Robb	Timothy Murphy	

Captain James Knox's Company

Capt.	James Knox	David Bryan
Lt.	James Craig	James Little
Lt.	Wm. Lovely	Joseph Smith
Sgt.	Wm. Scott	Wm. Flynn
Sgt.	Ben Powels	Ben Jennings
Sgt.	Joseph Pyles	David Critchlowe
Cpl.	Abraham McClean	John Croe
Cpl.	Francis Seaton	Dennis Croe
Cpl.	Jacob Shedicker	James Stacy
	Harkinson Ashby	Abraham Milhousen
	Joseph Batton	Amos Augustine
	Absalom Little	James Critchlowe
	John Free	Robert Caswell
	Robert Davidson	David McMahon
	Henry Smith	Thomas McMullin
	Wm. Garriott	James Allen
	Ben Jones	Daniel Thorp
	Martin Johnston	Shad Buttler
	Wm. Henson	Wm. Breadlove
	Reuben Easthin	Thomas Gamble
	Samuel Williams	Lester Broughon
	Rueben Bryon	Joseph Crumwell
	Baylor Jennings	Thomas Craigan
	Person Williams	Martin Wyngate
	------- Flynn	Joseph Pancake
	James Taffe	Henry Miller
	Solomon Hendricks	Henry Wyser
	Wm. Countrey	John Hicks
	John Robinson	

Note: Captain James Parr's Company Roll is Missing

Captain William Henderson's Company

Capt.	William Henderson	Ambros Hord	Wm. Berry	
Lt.	Andrew Moor	Wm. Dews	James Bolt	
Lt.	James Culbertson	Benjamin Cox	Wm. Todd	
Ens.	Wm. Stevens	William Blackwell	Jesse Cobb	
Sgt.	Thomas Mitchel	Charles Allon	Wm. Lahhy	
Sgt.	John Brown	Wm. Burch		
Sgt.	James McBride	Wm. Bailey		
Sgt.	John Davis	Edward Rodgers		
Sgt.	Thomas Kinkaid	Wm. Edwards		
Cpl.	Samuel Callender	Henry Taylor		
Cpl.	------ Clark	John Taylor		
Cpl.	Dudley Callawey	James Howard		
Cpl.	Samuel Failing	Waddy Vines		
	Richmond Dedman	Andrew Taylor		
	Joseph Lynn	Wm. Buttry		
	Mecjah Eaton	James Jones		
	Mathew Lettimor	Joseph Dunlap		
	Michael Oharro	Joseph Davis		
	Thomas Lockhard	Isiah Cruth		
	John Holt	Henry Iron		
	Wm. Bentsen	Thomas Madden		
	Thomas Patrick	John Diver		
	Wm. Hiland	Daniel Hiden		
	Eziriah Doss	John Humphry		
	Samuel Roundtree	Wm. Simon		
	John Porter	Archibald Lamb		
	Charles McGlachlin	David Street		
	Hendry Burley	Edward Casey		
	John Cockrin	Timothy Driskill		
	Thomas Carson	Peter Masie		
	Stephen Robertson	Wm. Furgison		
	Wm. McCorrmack	John Allon		
	Thomas Davis	Callot James		
	Peter Belf	Thomas Coleman		
	John Hastings	Thomas Burk		
	Wm. Haddle	Daniel Fitch		
	Jesse Howslee	John McCanless		
	George Smith	Jesse Rannalds		
	Joshua Orange	James Edmonton		

Captain Van Swearington's Company

Rank	Name		
Capt.	Van Swearington	Thomas Hood	John Pear
Lt.	B. Prather	Joseph Roggers	James Clark
Lt.	John Hardin	Thomas Cannoday	Con O Neal
Lt.	Alex Smith	Matthias Ward	John Corvin
Sgt.	John Lyon	John Fitzpatrick	Wm. Archer
Sgt.	James Morrison	Joseph Allen	Wm. Miller
Sgt.	John Askins	James Bodkin	John Deil
Sgt.	Samuel Phillies	Samuel Davice	John Lamb
Sgt.	Wm. Cary	Isaac Davice	Henry Jolly
Cpl.	John Wood	Daniel Shroenburg	Peter Young
Cpl.	Nathaniel Prather	John Hartness	John Tee
Cpl.	Jacob Warrington	Edward Hamon	Seth Stiles
	Robert Peter	Robert Moore	Wm. Owens
	Patrick Kelly	David Fitzgibbons	Wm. Carr
	Josiah Wilson	John McKuy	John Bags
	David Ferguson	Hugh Hamble	
	Thomas Guy	James Dunlap	
	Henry Cunningham	George Knox	
	James Thompson	James Birnes	
	Isaac Anderson	Edward Dehaven	
	John Herron	James Haslet	
	Hugh Forbus	Thomas Lyon	
	John Riley	James Murphy	
	Daniel Dever	John Dever	
	Archibald Pamer	Thomas Scott	
	Samuel Wilson	Michael Birk	
	John Miller	Lewis Hickman	
	Wm. Chaplin	David Devon	
	John Wilmore	John Rodgers	
	Neal McFetry	Thomas Dickerson	
	Phillip Young	Arthur Ingram	
	Thomas Bevinton	Henry Jolly	
	Henry Dickerson	Edward Bess	
	Benjamin Robbens	Thomas Sills	
	Nicholas Devour	Isaac Miller	
	James Birchfield	James French	
	John Diel	Thomas Montgomery	

Bibliography

Books

Abbatt, William. ed., *Memoirs of Major-General William Heath*. New York: William Abbatt, 1901.

Albion Robert and Leonidas Dodson, eds. *Philip Vickers Fithian: Journal , 1775-1776, Written on the Virginia-Pennsylvania Frontier and in the Army Around New York.* Princeton: Princeton University Press, 1934.

Babits, Lawrence E. *A Devil of a Whipping; The Battle of Cowpens.* Chapel Hill: University of North Carolina Press, 1998.

Ballagh, James C. ed., *Letters of Richard Henry Lee, Vol. 1.* New York : Macmillan Co., 1911.

Baxter, James ed. *The British Invasion from the North: Digby's Journal of the Campaigns of Generals Carleton and Burgoyne from Canada, 1776-1777.* New York: Da Capo Press, 1970.

Boatner III, Mark M. *Encyclopedia of the American Revolution.* 3rd ed., Stanpole Books, 1994.

Bodle, Wayne. *The Valley Forge Winter: Civilians and Soldiers in War.* PA: Pennsylvania State University Press, 2002.

Borick, Carl P. *A Gallant Defense: The Siege of Charleston, 1780.* University of South Carolina Press, 2003

Boyd, Julian, ed. *The Papers Thomas Jefferson.*
Vol. 3-6, Princeton, NJ: Princeton University Press,
1951.

Boyle, Joseph Lee. *Writings from the Valley Forge
Encampment of the Continental Army.* Vol. 1-2
Bowie:Heritage Books Inc., 2000.

Brown, Lloyd A. & Howard H. Peckman ed. *Revolutionary
War Journals of Henry Dearborn: 1775-1783.*
Freeport, NY: Books for Libraries Press, 1939.

Buchanan, John. *The Road to Guilford Courthouse: The
American Revolution in the Carolina.* NY: John Wiley
& Sons, Inc., 1997

Burgoyne, John. *A State of the Expedition from Canada.*
New York Times & Arno Press, 1969.

Campbell, Charles. *The Orderly Book of that Portion of the
American Army stationed at or near Williamsburg,
Virginia under the command of General Andrew
Lewis, from March 18th, 1776 to August 20th, 1776.*
Richmond, VA: 1860.

Carrington, Henry B. *Battles of the American Revolution.*
New York: A. S. Barnes & Co., 1877.

Cecere, Michael. *An Officer of Very Extraordinary Merit:
Charles Porterfield and the American War for
Independence, 1775-1780.* Westminster, MD:
Heritage Books, 2004

Cecere, Michael. *Captain Thomas Posey and the 7th Virginia
Regiment.* Westminster, MD: Heritage Books, 2005

Cecere, Michael. *They Behaved Like Soldiers: Captain John Chilton and the Third Virginia Regiment.* Westminster, MD: Heritage Books, 2004

Chase, Philander D. ed. *The Papers of George Washington: Revolutionary War Series.* Charlottesville: University Press of Virginia, 2000.

Clark, William, ed. *Naval Documents of the American Revolution, Vol. 5.* Washington: 1970.

Commager, Henry and Richard Morris, ed. "Journal of Captain Allen McLane, 15 July, 1779," *The Spirit of 'Seventy-Six: The Story of the American Revolution as Told by Participants.* NY: Castle Books, 1967.

Cook, Frederick. ed. *Journals of the Military Expedition of Major General John Sullivan Against the Six Nations of Indians in 1779.* Freeport, NY: Books for Library Press, 1887.

Conrad, Dennis M. *The Papers of General Nathanael Greene, Vol. 9-11.* Chapel Hill: University of North Carolina Press, 1997-2000.

Cullen, Charles and Herbert Johnson, ed. *The Papers of John Marshall, Vol. 1.* Chapel Hill : Univ. of NC Press, 1974

Dandridge, Danske. "Henry Bedinger to --- Findley", *Historic Sheperdstown.* Charlottesville, VA: Michie Co., 1910.

Dann, John C. *The Revolution Remembered: Eyewitness Accounts of the War Independence.* Chicago: University of Chicago Press, 1980.

Dawson, Henry B. "General Daniel Morgan: An Autobiography," *The Historical Magazine and Notes and Queries Concerning the Antiquities, History and Biography of America. 2nd Series, Vol. 9.* Morrisania, NY, 1871.

Dorman, John Frederick. *Virginia Revolutionary Pension Applications, Volumes 1-52.* Washington D.C., 1958-1995.

Draper, Lyman C. *King's Mountain and Its Heroes: History of the Battle of King's Mountain.* Cincinnati: Peter G. Thomson, 1881.

Ewald, Captain Johann. *Diary of the American War: A Hessian Journal.* New Haven: Yale Univ. Press, 1979. Translated & edited by Joseph Tustin

Fischer, David Hackett. *Washington's Crossing.* Oxford University Press, 2004.

Fitzpatrick, John C. *The Writings of George Washington from the Original Manuscripts, 1745-1799.* Washington: U.S. Govt. Printing Office, 1931.

Flickinger, Floyd B. "Diary of Lieutenant William Heth while a Prisoner in Quebec, 1776," *Annual Papers of Winchester Virginia Historical Society, Vol. 1,* 1931.

Flickinger, Floyd B. "Captain Morgan and His Riflemen," *Winchester-Frederick County Historical Society, Vol. 14.* 2002.

Force, Peter, ed., *American Archives: 5th Series.* Washington D.C.: U.S. Congress, 1848-1853.

Graham, James. *The Life of General Daniel Morgan.*
Bloomingburg, NY: Zebrowski Historical Services,
1993. Press of Virginia, 1965.

Hatch, Robert. *Thrust for Canada: The American Attempt on
Quebec in 1775-76.* Boston: Houghton Mifflin, 1979.

Hening, William. *The Statutes at Large Being a Collection of
all the Laws of Virginia, Vol. 9.* Richmond: J & G
Cochran, 1821.

Higginbotham, Don. *Daniel Morgan: Revolutionary
Rifleman.* Chapel Hill: Univeristy of North
Carolina Press, 1961.

Hinrichs, Captain Johann. *The Siege of Charleson: Diaries
and Letters of Hessian Officers.* Ann Arbor:
University of Michigan Press, 1938.
Trans. & ed. Bernhard A. Uhlendorf,

Jackman, Sydney ed. *With Burgoyne from Quebec: An
Account of the Life at Quebec and of the Famous
Battle at Saratoga.* Toronto: Macmillan of Canada,
1963.
*Note: First published as volume one of Travels Through the Interior Parts
of North America, by Thomas Anburey*

Jackson, John W. *Valley Forge: Pinnacle of Courage.*
Gettysburg, PA: Thomas Publications, 1992.

Johnston, Henry P. *The Battle of Harlem Heights.* London:
Macmillian, 1897.

Johnson, Henry P. *The Campaign of 1776 Around New York
and Brooklyn.* New York: Da Capa Press, 1971.

Jones, Alfred E. *The Journal of Alexander Chesney, A South Carolina Loyalist in the Revolution and After*. Ohio State University, 1921.

Kapp, Friedrich. *The Life of Frederick William von Steuben*. NY: Corner House Historical Publications, 1999. (Originally published in 1859)

Ketchum, Richard M. *Saratoga: Turning Point of America's Revolutionary War*. New York: Holt & Co., 1997.

LaCrosse Jr., Richard B. *The Frontier Rifleman*. Union City, TN: Pioneer Press, 1989.

LaCrosse Jr., Richard B. *Revolutionary Rangers: Daniel Morgan's Riflemen and Their Role on the Northern Frontier*. Bowie, MD: Heritage Books, 2002.

Lamb, Roger. *An Original and Authentic Journal of Occurrences During the Late American War from Its Commencement to 1783*. Dublin: Wilkinson & Courtney, 1809.

Lee, Charles. *The Lee Papers, Vol. 1*. Collections of the New York Historical Society, 1871.

Lee, Henry. *The Revolutionary War Memoirs of General Henry Lee*. New York: Da Capo Press, 1998. Originally Published in 1812

Lesser, Charles H. ed. *The Sinews of Independence: Monthly Strength Reports of the Continental Army*. Chicago: The Univiversity of Chicago Press, 1976.

Lowell, Edward J. *Letters and Memoirs Relating to the War of American Independence and the Capture of the German Troops at Saratoga.* Williamstown, MA: Corner House Publishers, 1975.

Luzader, John. *Decision on the Hudson: The Battles of Saratoga. Eastern National, 2002.*

Marshall, John. *The Life of George Washington, Vol. 2.* Fredericksburg, VA: The Citizens' Guild of Washington's Boyhood Home, 1926.

Martin, David. *The Philadelphia Campaign, June 1777 – July 1778.* Da Capa Press, 1993.

McGuire, Thomas. *The Surprise of Germantown, October 4, 1777.* Cliveden of the National Trust for Historic Preservation and Thomas Publications, 1994.

McIlwaine, H.R. ed. *Journals of the Council of the State of Virginia, Vol. 1.* Richmond: Virginia State Library, 1931.

Mintz, Max M. *Seeds of Empire: The American Revolutionary Conquest of the Iroquois.* New York: New York University Press, 1999.

Morrissey, Brendan. *Quebec 1775: The American invasion of Canada..* Osprey Publishing, 2003.

Morrissey, Brendan. *Saratoga 1777: Turning Point of the Revolution.* Osprey Publishing, 2000.

Moore, Frank. *Diary of the American Revolution, from Newspapers and Original Documents.* 2 vols. New York:Charles Schibner, 1860. Reprint. New York: New York Times & Arno Press, 1969.

Mowday, Bruce E. *September 11, 1777, Washington's Defeat at Brandywine Dooms Philadelphia.* Shippensburg, PA: White Mane Books, 2002.

O'Kelly, Patrick. *Nothing But Blood and Slaughter: The Revolutionary War in the Carolinas.* Blue House Tavern Press, 2004.

Palmer, William ed. *Calendar of Virginia State Papers.* Vol. 1-2, Richmond: R.F. Walker, 1875.

Posey, John Thornton. *General Thomas Posey: Son of the American Revolution.* East Lansing: Michigan State Univ. Press, 1992.

Pausch, George. *Journal of Captain Pausch, Chief of the Hanau Artillery During the Burgoyne Campaign.* Albany, NY: Joel Munsell's Sons, 1886. Translated by William L. Stone.

Powell, Robert. "David Griffith to Major Powell, May 28, 1777," *Biographical Sketch of Col. Levin Powell, 1737-1810: Including his Correspondence during the Revolutionary War.* Alexandria, Virginia: G.H. Ramey & Son, 1877.

Reed, John F. *Campaign to Valley Forge: July 1, 1777 – December 19, 1777.* Pioneer Press, 1980.

Riedesel, Madam. *Letters and Memoirs Relating to the War of American Independence and the Capture of the German Troops at Saratoga.* New York: G. & C. Carvill, 1827.

Roberts, John M. ed. *Autobiography of a Revolutionary Soldier.* New York: Arno Press, 1979. Originally published in 1859

Roberts, Kenneth. *March to Quebec: Journals of the Members of Arnold's Expedition.* New York: Country Life Press, 1938.

Rodney, Caesar. *The Diary of Captain Thomas Rodney, 1776-1777.* Wilmington: The Historical Society of Delaware, 1888.

Rogers, Horatio ed. *Hadden's Journal and Orderly Book: A Journal Kept in Canada and Upon Burgoyne's Campaign in 1776 and 1777.* Boston: Gregg Press, 1972.

Russell, T. Tripplett and John K. Gott. *Fauquier County in the Revolution.* Westminster, MD : Willow Bend Books, 1988.

Ryan, Dennis P. "Robert Beale Memoirs," *A Salute to Courage: The American Revolution as Seen Through Wartime Writings of Officers of the Continental Army and Navy.* New York: Columbia University Press, 1979.

Saffell, W.T.R. *Records of the Revolutionary War*, 3rd ed. Baltimore: Charles Saffell, 1894.

Sanchez-Saavedra, E.M. *A Guide to Virginia Military Organizations in the American Revolution, 1774-1787*. Westminster, MD: Willow Bend Books, 1978.

Scheer, George F., and Hugh F. Rankin. *Rebels & Redcoats: The American Revolution through the Eyes of Those Who Fought and Lived It*. New York: Da Capo Press, 1987.

Scribner, Robert L. and Tarter, Brent (comps). *Revolutionary Virginia: The Road to Independence, Volumes 1-7*. Charlottesville: University Press of Virginia, 1978.

Selby, John E. *The Revolution in Virginia : 1775-1783*. New York : Holt Inc., 1996.

Sellers, John R. *The Virginia Continental Line*. Williamsburg: The Virginia Bicentennial Commission, 1978.

Simcoe, Lt. Col. John. *Simcoe's Military Jouirnal: A History of the Operations of a Partisan Corps Called the Queen's Rangers, Commanded by Lieut. Col. J. G. Simcoe, During the War of Revolution*. New York: New York Times and Arno Press, 1968.

Smith, Jean Edward. *John Marshall : Definer of a Nation*. New York : Holt Inc., 1996.

Smith, Samuel. *The Battle of Brandywine*. Monmouth Beach, NJ: Philip Freneau Press, 1976.

Sparks, Jared ed. *The Correspondence of the American Revolution being Letters of Eminent Men to George Washington, Vol. 2*. Boston : Little, Brown & Co., 1853.

Stille, Charles. *Major-General Anthony Wayne and the Pennsylvania Line in the Continental Army*. Port Washington, NY: Kenniket Press, Inc., 1968. First published in 1893

Stryker, William. *The Battle of Monmouth*. Princeton: Princeton University Press, 1927.

Symonds, Craig L. *A Battlefield ATLAS of the American Revolution*. The Nautical & Aviation Publishing Co. of America Inc., 1986.

Taaffe, Stephen R. *The Philadelphia Campaign, 1777-1778*. University of Kansas Press, 2003.

Tarleton, Banastre. *A History of the Campaigns of 1780-1781 in the Southern Provinces of North America*. NH: AYER Company, 1999. Originally printed in 1787

Tarter, Brent and Robert Scribner, ed. *Revolutionary Virginia: The Road to Independence, Vol. 1-7*. University Press of Virginia, 1983.

Thacher, James. *A Military Journal during the American Revolutionary War*. Hartford: CT, S. Andrus and Son, 1854. Reprint, New York: Arno Press, 1969.

Tharp, Louise Hall. *The Baroness and the General*. Boston: Little, Brown & Co., 1962.

Townsend, Joseph. "Some Account of the British Army under the Command of General Howe, and of the Battle of Brandywine," *Eyewitness Accounts of the American Revolution*. New York: Arno Press, 1969.

Uhlendorf, Bernhard A. ed. & trans. *The Siege of Charleston: With an Account of the Province of South Carolina: Diaries and Letters of Hessian Officers*. Ann Arbor, MI: University of Michigan Press, 1938.

Ward, Henry M. *Duty, Honor, or Country: General George Weedon and the American Revolution*. Philadelphia: American Philosophical Society, 1979.

Wilkinson, James. *Memoirs of My Own Times, Vol. 1* Philadelphia: Abraham Small, 1816
Reprinted by AMS Press Inc., :NY, 1973

Ward, Harry M. *Duty, Honor, or Country : General George* Weedon and the American Revolution. *Philadelphia :* American Philosophical Society, 1979.

Wasmus, J.F. *An Eyewitness Account of the American Revolution and New England Life: The Journal of J.F. Wasmus, German Company Surgeon, 1776-1783*. NY: Greenwood Press, 1990.
Translated by Helga Doblin

Willard, Margaret. ed., *Letters of the American Revolution: 1774-1776*. Boston & New York: Houghton Mifflin Co., 1925

Wright, Robert K. *The Continental Army*. Washington, D.C. Center of Military History: United States Army, 1989.

----------- *Journals of the Continental Congress*. Library of Congress Online at www.loc.gov.

---------- *Narrative of Johann Carl Buettner in the American Revolution*. New York: Benjamin Bloom, 1971.

-------- *Public Papers of George Clinton: First Governor of New York, Vol. 3*. Albany: State Printer, 1900.

Periodicals

Boyle, Joseph Lee. "From Saratoga to Valley Forge: The Diary of Lt. Samuel Armstrong," *The Pennsylvania Magazine of History and Biography, Vol. 121, No. 3 July 1997.*

Dearborn, Henry. "A Narrative of the Saratoga Campaign – Major General Henry Dearborn, 1815," *The Bulletin of the Fort Ticonderoga Museum, Vol. 1 no. 5.* January, 1929.

Elmer, Ebenezer. "The Journal of Ebenezer Elmer," *The Pennsylvania Magazine of History and Biography.* Vol. 35 Philadelphia: Historical Society of Pennsylvania, 1911.

Gates, Horatio. "Horatio Gates, Major General, Commanding Southern Army. Letters and Orders from June 21 to August 31, 1780", *Magazine of American History, Vol. 5, No. 4*, October, 1880

Heth, William. "Orderly Book of Major William Heth of the Third (sic) Virginia regiment, May 15 – July 1, 1777", *Virginia Historical Society Collections, New Series, 11*, 1892.

Jordan, John W. ed., "Bethleham During the Revolution." *Pennsylvania Magazine of History and Biography, Vol. 12,* 1888.

Katcher, Philip. "They Behaved Like Soldiers: The Third Virginia Regiment at Harlem Heights", *Virginia Cavalcade*, Vol. 26, No. 2, Autumn 1976.

McMichael, James. "The Diary of Lt. James McMichael of the Pennsylvania Line, 1776-1778," *The Pennsylvania Magazine of History and Biography*. Vol. 16, no. 2, 1892.

Montresor, John. "Journal of Captain John Montresor," *The Pennsylvania Magazine of History and Biography. Vol. 5*. Philadelphia: The Historical Society of Pennsylvania, 1881

Porterfield, Charles. "Diary of Colonel Charles Porterfield," *Magazine of American History, Vol. 21*. April 1889.

Schnitzer, Eric. "Battling for the Saratoga Landscape," *Cultural Landscape Report: Saratoga Battle, Saratoga National Park*, Vol. 1, Boston, MA: Olmsted Center for Landscape Preservation.

Sergeant R. "The Battle of Princeton," *The Pennsylvania Magazine of History and Biography, Vol. 20, No. 1.* 1896.

Seymour, William. "Journal of the Southern Expedition, 1780-1783", *The Pennsylvania Magazine of History and* Biography, Vol. 7. 1883.

Sullivan, Thomas. "Before and After the Battle of Brandywine: Extracts from the Journal of Sergeant Thomas Sullivan of H.M. Forty-Ninth Regiment of Foot," *The Pennsylvania Magazine of History and Biography*. Vol 31, Philadelphia: Historical Society of Pennsylvania, 1907.

Tyler, Lyon. "The Old Virginia Line in the Middle States During the American Revolution," *Tyler's Quarterly Historical and Genealogical Magazine: Vol.12.* Richmond, VA: Richmond Press Inc., 1931.

Waddell, J.A. " Diary of a Prisoner of War at Quebec, 1776," *Virginia Magazine of History and Biography, Vol. 9.* Richmond, VA: The Virginia Historical Society, July, 1901

"Actions at Brandywine and Paoli, Described by a British Officer," *The Pennsylvania Magazine of History and Biography.* Vol. 24, Philadelphia: Historical Society of *Pennsylvania, 1905.*

"King's Mountain Expedition," *An Annual Publication of Historical Papers: Governor W.W. Holden and Revolutionary Documents, Series 3.* Durham, NC: Historical Society of Trinity College, 1899.

"Personal Recollections of Captain Enoch Anderson, an Officer of the Delaware Regiment in the Revolutionary War," *Papers of the Historical Society of Delaware, Vol. 16.* Wilmington: The Historical Society of Delaware, 1896.

Unpublished Works

Butler, Lieutenant Colonel Richard to Col. James Wilson, 22 January, 1778 Gratz Collection, Case 4, Box 11, Historical Society of Pennsylvania.

Filipski, Jim and Steve Collward. *A Chronology of the Appointment & Commands of Captain Antoni Selin and His Association with the Independent Corps of Captain John Paul Schott, Major Nicholas de Ottendorf and Col. Charles Armand.* Accessed via www.captainselinscompany.org/chronology.html

Goodwin, Mary. *Clothing and Accoutrements of the Officers and Soldiers of the Virginia Forces: 1775-1780.* 1962

Heth, William. "Orderly Book of Major William Heth of the Third (sic) Virginia Regiment, May 15 – July 1, 1777", *Virginia Historical Society Collections.* New Series, 11 1892.
Note: This orderly book is incorrectly titled and is actually the orderly book of Daniel Morgan's 11th Virginia Regiment.

Orderly Book of Captain Robert Gamble of the Second Virginia Regiment, Commanded by Colonel Christian Febiger, August 21 – November 16, 1779
Accessed via www.ls.net/~newriver/va/gamble1.html

Orderly Book of the Company of Captain George Stubblefield, Fifth Virginia Regiment From March 3 to July 10, 1776.
Accessed via www.revwar75.com

222

Posey, Thomas. "*A Short Biography of the Life of Governor Thomas Posey,*" Thomas Posey Papers. Indiana *Historical Society Library, Indianapolis, IN.*

Posey, Thomas, *Revolutionary War Journal,* Thomas Posey Papers, Indiana Historical Society Library, Indianapolis, IN

Weedon, George. *Correspondence Account of the Battle of Brandywine, 11 September, 1777.* The original manuscript is in the collections of the Chicago Historical Society, Transcribed by Bob McDonald, 2001.

Index

225

226

About the Author

Michael Cecere Sr. is the proud father of two wonderful children, Jenny and Michael Jr., and the grateful husband of Susan Cecere. He teaches American History at Robert E. Lee High School in Fairfax County, Virginia (full-time) and at Northern Virginia Community College (part-time). He holds a Master of Arts Degree from the University of Akron in History and another in Political Science. An avid Revolutionary and Civil War re-enactor, he is a member of the 3rd and 7th Virginia Regiments and the Liberty Rifles, and participates in numerous living history events throughout the year. *They Are Indeed a Very Useful Corps* is his fourth book. His earlier books, entitled, *They Behaved Like Soldiers: Captain John Chilton and the Third Virginia Regiment, An Officer of Very Extraordinary Merit: Charles Porterfield and the American War for Independence, 1775-1780,* and *Captain Thomas Posey and the 7th Virginia Regiment,* provide insight into the lives of these officers and their units. He is currently conducting research on northern Virginia's role in the Revolution.

4348430

Made in the USA
Charleston, SC
06 January 2010